school success
for kids with
Dyslexia
& other reading difficulties

school success
for kids with
Dyslexia
& other reading difficulties

Walter E. Dunson, Ph.D.

PRUFROCK PRESS INC.

WACO, TEXAS

Library of Congress Cataloging-in-Publication Data

Dunson, Walter E.
School success for kids with dyslexia and other reading difficulties / by Walter E. Dunson.
p. cm.
Includes bibliographical references.
ISBN 978-1-59363-962-4 (pbk.)
1. Dyslexic children--Education. 2. Learning disabled children--Education. 3. Reading--Remedial teaching. I. Title.
LC4708.D86 2012
371.91'44--dc23
          2012016060

Edited by Lacy Compton

Production design by Raquel Trevino

ISBN-13: 978-1-59363-962-4

Printed in the United States of America.

At the time of this book's publication, all facts and figures cited are the most current available. All telephone numbers, addresses, and website URLs are accurate and active. All publications, organizations, websites, and other resources exist as described in the book, and all have been verified. The author and Prufrock Press Inc. make no warranty or guarantee concerning the information and materials given out by organizations or content found at websites, and we are not responsible for any changes that occur after this book's publication. If you find an error, please contact Prufrock Press Inc.

Prufrock Press Inc.
P.O. Box 8813
Waco, TX 76714-8813
Phone: (800) 998-2208
Fax: (800) 240-0333
http://www.prufrock.com

v

Contents

Introduction

N O academic skill is more vital than the ability to read (Edmonds et al., 2009). Without reading skills, the chances for an individual's academic and occupational success are limited (Lyon, 1998b). As proof, we merely need to engage in a rudimentary investigation to discover that reading disabilities have a tremendous social impact.

A research study conducted by the Pew Research Center indicated that at the end of 2007, more than one in every 100 adults was confined in an American jail or prison (Pew Center on the States, 2008). According to figures gathered and analyzed by the Pew Public Safety Performance Project, in total, approximately 7,300,000 United States citizens were either in jail, in prison, on probation, or on parole. Translated, that is one out of every 31 American adults (Pew Center on the States, 2008). Additionally, the United States has 5% of the world's population but 25% of the world's prison inmates (Loury & Western, 2010). Why is this information significant in terms of reading? Because further research demonstrates that three-fourths of those incarcerated have not graduated from high school and a staggering 70% are functionally illiterate and read below a fourth-grade level (Barton, 2011). These figures are a clear indication that reading instruction in American educational institutions is problematic.

This is directly related to the nature and structure of American educational institutions where inadequate instruction in phonemic awareness and basic spelling rules leads to the development of inadequate code-breaking skills, which translates into the creation of a disability in basic reading skills.

A disability in basic reading skills is primarily caused by deficits in phonological awareness, which is independent of any achievement capacity (Lyon, 1998b). More clearly stated, reading disability has no connection with learning capacity or intelligence. Further, deficits in phonological awareness can be identified in late kindergarten and first grade using inexpensive, straightforward testing protocol, and these deficits can be remediated using a systematic approach to breaking the English code. This book takes that systematic approach and breaks it down for parents and teachers, while presenting some basic information on dyslexia and other reading difficulties and general strategies that can be used to improve students' reading skills.

How to Use This Book

The primary objective of *School Success for Kids With Dyslexia and Other Reading Difficulties* is to provide parents and teachers with goals and a structured approach that will meet the needs of students requiring either primary instruction or remediation in the decoding and encoding of the English language.

This work provides a systematic and forensic approach to mastering the English language and a solid foundation for reading, writing, and spelling skills for students who are struggling with language acquisition. With this forensic approach, students can be shown the phonetic nature of the English language and the proper structure of the written language.

This book was written for use by dedicated parents and by teachers, educational specialists, language specialists, and mainstream or special needs English departments. If a departmental approach is used, it is recommended that the department nominate one individual, preferably one who is trained in the Orton-Gillingham approach, to evaluate the appropriateness of its application and to make determinations concerning its continued usage. This guide should be presented at the pace determined by the presenter, whose determination should be based solely upon the mastery level of the student.

The system herein has been organized to provide fluidity of information to ensure success. Concepts that build upon other concepts have been placed accordingly. Although some of the presentations may seem repetitious, this commonly utilized method enhances the students' exposure to foreign concepts and fosters mastery.

I am aware that throughout this book, I have included information that crosses the line into the arena of speech pathology. I do this in order to familiarize those who have not had the exposure to speech pathology that I have received over my 27-year career. The information that I have gained over this period of time has served to strengthen my grasp of the articulation process and its inseparable relationship to phonemic awareness. In order to pass this information on to struggling students so that they may receive the full benefit of language remediation, parents and teachers themselves must become familiar with the process of articulation and its inseparable relationship to phonemic awareness. The phonemic details that permeate this book will serve as this resource.

You will find as you progress through this work that there are no cute little animals, funny faces, games, or anything else to distract the student from the task at hand. This curriculum is not designed to entertain. With this book, I merely seek to explicitly and systematically teach the intrinsic relationship between sounds and the symbols that represent them in the English code.

As we proceed with helping remediate the language and reading skills of our students, remember the words of the novelist Marcel Proust, who wrote:

"The real voyage of discovery
consists not in seeking new landscapes . . .
. . . but in having new eyes."

Let us move forward and develop our new eyes.

chapter 1

The Development of Reading Skills

THE most fundamental responsibility of schools is to teach students how to read (Moats, 1999). The development of reading skills obviously serves as the gateway to the world of printed information, as reading serves as the major foundational skill for all school-based learning (Lyon, 1998a). Most, if not all, of the informal education that we receive is accomplished without the use of printed material. Historically, the oral tradition was the foundation of the informal education process and continues to remain so. However, school presents a different situation—formal education in school requires the ability to read printed material. Through the development of reading skills, we prepare ourselves for our journey toward learning the material that must be mastered during the formal education process.

Many proponents of "whole language" education feel that because humans learn to speak their native language through immersion, the act of reading follows a similar pattern and exposure to the printed word leads to the development of reading skills. This reasoning bears a false truth value. A great deal of care and attention to detail must accompany reading instruction, because reading is quite different from speech.

In speech, the listener is provided with many clues as to the meaning of the words presented by the speaker. Intonation, pitch, cadence, and body language all provide context clues that assist in the comprehension of auditory signals. Further, according to the innateness hypothesis, children are equipped with a blueprint for the innate principles and properties that pertain to the grammars of all spoken human language, called *universal grammar* (Fromkin, Hyams, & Rodman, 2002). Barring neurologically-based developmental delays, children do not require explicit instruction to master the spoken language. Universal grammar aids the child in the task of constructing spoken language. Additionally, through stages in oral communication, a speaker learns from the surrounding linguistic environment the proper cadence, pitch, and intonation associated with the successful display of language ability as well as the rules of grammar that are language specific. This presents speech as a natural process (Fromkin et al., 2002).

Reading involves a quite different presentation for a couple of reasons. First, written language is a relatively recent human construct. In the evolution of writing, we have designated symbols to represent the sounds of spoken language. We have, in essence, created our own code. The sound-symbol correspondence that has been developed for the English language is called the *English code*. Students must absolutely understand the sounds of our language and the symbols that represent them. Our spoken language has a code, and written language, as a representation of spoken language, therefore must also have a code. The code for written language is more complex because most visual and auditory cues must be inferred based upon two-dimensional symbolic representations called *punctuation*.

Although universal grammar was specified for spoken language, written language is of a different construct. Education, based upon its modern manifestation, is founded upon mastery of the written language. Just as children learned the rules for spoken language through oral communication, they must learn the rules for written language. In order to read, a student must be able to translate the written symbol to the corresponding sound that it represents. To spell, students must be able to translate the sound to the appropriate written symbol that represents it. This knowledge is called *sound-symbol correspondence*. The ability to make this translation is called *phonemic awareness*. Reading, or decoding, involves sound-symbol correspondence and phonemic awareness, neither of which is a naturally occurring process. Further, students should be taught not only the phonemes (sounds) and graphemes (letters) associated with the language, but also the myriad of spelling rules governing usage and application. For example, when choosing between using "ai" and "ay," for graphically representing the / $\bar{a}$ / phoneme within a spoken word, the rule depends upon the location of the long vowel phoneme within the word. If the long vowel phoneme / $\bar{a}$ / appears in the middle of the word, we use "ai" (e.g., "rain," "chain," "pail"). If, however, the long vowel phoneme / $\bar{a}$ / appears at the end of the pronounced word, we use "ay" (e.g., "day," "pay," "stay").

Second, the two key components of reading, which do not manifest themselves in speech, are *word identification* and *concept imagery*. Word identification involves recognizing that words are a systematic string of individual graphemes or letters. Each individual sequential combination represents a different word. Students must be able to string together the individual phonemes or sounds the letters represent to produce these words. This is the essence of decoding. The other half of the reading puzzle involves comprehension of the meanings behind the sequential combinations of letters, or words. Concept imagery allows students to visualize the item or process represented by the words. Students who have weak word attack skills (word identification) will stumble and stammer as they attempt to read the printed language. Those weak in concept imagery (comprehension) may read with prosody but will not understand what is read.

To understand the impact of word identification and concept imagery on the reading process, one merely needs to be reminded that the printed language is a code for spoken language.

Word Identification

Every spoken language has a class of vowels and a class of consonants (see Chapter 4 for more information; Fromkin et al., 2002). The essence of decoding, as mentioned earlier, is to translate the written symbol to the corresponding sound that it represents. Additionally, a student must string together the individual sounds or phonemes to produce a word. Sound-symbol correspondence is paramount. A student must recognize the symbol, and he or she must have knowledge of what the symbol represents. Take a look at Figure 1. Read it out loud.

The overwhelming majority of us cannot decipher what we see in Figure 1 because we do not recognize the symbols. Even if we did recognize the symbols, do we know what sound or sounds each symbol represents? This is knowledge that we must have, as we must be able to string the sounds together in order to produce a word. Now, try reading the passage in Figure 2.

Languages, written and spoken, have grammars that govern their construction (e.g., subject and verb, interrogatives). All grammars contain rules of a similar kind for the formation of words and sentences (Fromkin et al., 2002). In the example in Figure 2, even though we recognize the symbols, we are unable to string together the represented phonemes into words. Note that we have a mixture of alphabetic and numeric symbols. The sequence "hrt5n," for example, is inconsistent with how our code manifests.

Concept Imagery

In the final figure, Figure 3, each sequence of symbols manifests in the fashion to which we are accustomed in our language. Note that we have a capital letter at the beginning of each sequence and punctuation at the end. What separates the two sequences is that we have comprehension of the meanings behind the sequential combinations

ӿϘϙϚϛϜϝ∿ͻЩϲϙϗʈϯϭϬϪϏϐϩϥϤШϳjΘϵϷϸϹϺρϽϹ ϿЀЁЂВВЦҮЙКЋЊЉ ЃДЖЗЙИЛПЦЧЪЮЖѲҍЛӇНМҁҹЏҨГҌҔҝҞҌЫЙГҪѿѼҞҶ ѤҌҪ

Figure 1. **Try to read this out loud.**

Jn hrt5n fjjnm wedc ddn djdunasp jjumsn kk,l sueyhh ssfd. Kooplp een-bddvc, ury, urrjqq haas nikko ;pplo nsx kkiedd ido dppp9 kkdd dd. Yyt, u.

Figure 2. **Now, try reading this.**

1. Tol neddim az nilp ju klyr geed voj serfew molg aq ik loi me. Huy ge, wys.
2. Mary had a little lamb. Its fleece was white as snow.

Figure 3. **Two examples of sequences of symbols.**

of letters (words) in sequence #2. We are able to "pull meaning from the print."

For additional clarity, concept imagery is the ability to form an image in the mind's eye based solely upon sensory input, whether visual, auditory, or tactile-kinesthetic. It represents the ability to take the next logical step toward comprehension. For example, if I say that the animal I am thinking of has whiskers, four paws, a tail, and says, "meow," you envision a cat. You formed an image in the mind's eye based solely upon the sensory input. Students with strong word identification and poor concept imagery skills may read beautifully. Yet, ask them what they have just read, and they will respond with "I don't know." Academic language therapy is the proper treatment for weak word identification. To address weakness in concept imagery, I recommend that parents investigate the curriculum *Visualizing and Verbalizing for Language Comprehension and Thinking* by the Lindamood-Bell Learning Process company.

The National Reading Panel

In 1997, the United States Congress asked Dr. G. Reid Lyon, Chief of the National Institute of Child Health and Human Development, National Institutes of Health, to appoint a 14-member panel of experts to determine the effectiveness of various approaches to reading instruction. The criteria for the selection of individuals for the panel included the ability to be completely objective as the panel researched and evaluated more than 100,000 different reading programs and methodologies. Better stated, no member of the panel could have any investment, financial or otherwise, with any reading methodology or program. The National Reading Panel Report (Learning Point Associates, 2004) condensed several decades of scientific research and showed that effective reading instruction should address five critical areas, labeled as the five pillars of reading. They are:

1. phonological awareness,

2. phonics,

3. fluency,

4. vocabulary, and

5. comprehension.

Phonological Awareness/Phonics

To begin, many believe that phonological (phonemic) awareness and phonics are the same thing. Nothing could be further from the truth. Phonemic awareness is the awareness that words are composed of sequences or strings of individual sounds called *phonemes*. Phonemes are the smallest parts of sound in a spoken word. For example, the word "at" has two sounds or phonemes, / ă / / t /. The word "dog" has three phonemes, / d / / ŏ / / g /. Even though the word "box" has three letters, it has four phonemes, / b / / ŏ / / k / / s /. As evidenced by the word "box," phonemes are completely separate entities from the symbols that we call letters of the alphabet or *graphemes*. A grapheme is the smallest part of written language that represents a phoneme in the spelling of a word. A grapheme may be just one letter such as "t" or "d" or several letters such as "aw" or "eigh." Graphemes represent the phonemes in written language.

Students must have the ability to identify and visually imagine the number, order, and identity of sounds and letters within words. These abilities underlie accurate word attack, word recognition, reading fluency, and spelling. Children who have phonemic awareness skills are likely to have an easier time learning to read and spell than children who have few or none of these skills. Weakness in these functions causes individuals to add, omit, substitute, and reverse sounds and letters within words while reading and spelling.

The five key skills that serve as the foundation of phonemic awareness are:

- **phoneme replication:** the ability to repeat a sound that one hears;

- **blending:** the ability to join a string of phonemes together to create a word;

- **segmenting:** the ability to break a word into its individual phonemes;

- **substitution:** the ability to replace a phoneme with a new phoneme, creating a new word; and

- **rhyming:** the ability to find words with the same rhyme[1].

Phonics, on the other hand, is the study of the predictable relationship between the phonemes or sounds in our language and the graphemes or letters that we use to represent these sounds. The purpose of phonics instruction is to teach children the sound-symbol relationships and how to use those relationships to read words. To achieve this, pho-

---

1   The *onset* is the beginning of the word, usually consisting of consonants. The *rhyme* (rime) is the rest of the word without the initial consonant structure (i.e., single consonant, consonant digraph, or consonant blend). For example, in the word "rest," the consonant "r" is the onset. The remaining letters in the word, "est," create the rhyme. Words that end with the phonemes / ĕ / / s / / t / rhyme with "rest" (e.g., "test," "guest," "blessed").

nics instruction must be explicit and systematic. It is explicit in that sound-symbol relationships are directly taught. Students are told, for example, that the letter "s" stands for the / s / sound; however, when the letter "s" sits between two vowels or follows a voiced sound, it says / z /. Phonics instruction is systematic in that it follows a scope and sequence that allows children to form and read words early on. The skills taught are constantly reviewed and applied to real reading.

Fluency

Fluency is the ability to read text accurately and quickly with expression. Embedded in this is the notion of reading with proper pitch and cadence as dictated by punctuation. Fluency is aided by the rapid recognition of high-frequency words and the usage of meaning, structure, and visual cues to self-correct.

Vocabulary

Vocabulary is important for comprehension. Readers can't understand what they read without knowing what most words mean. The most profitable and enduring manner through which to strengthen vocabulary skills is to teach students to use word structure to determine meaning. As discussed in Chapter 5, English Language Word Construction, the English language is composed of a mixture of other linguistic influences. Here, the linguistic influences come in the form of how we construct the words that compose our spoken and written language. The three main linguistic models of word construction that constitute the English language are Latinate word construction (55%), Anglo-Saxon word construction (25%), and Greek word construction (11%). In order to successfully master our language, students must receive adequate exposure to the components of each of these three linguistic influences. This includes the foundational roots of Latinate word construction and the combining forms (roots) of Greek word construction. Additionally, students should be encouraged to read a variety of grade-level texts to acquire new vocabulary through the identification of these Latinate roots and Greek combining forms in action.

Comprehension

Good readers are purposeful and active (Reading Rockets, 2012). They have a purpose for reading and monitor their reading to make sure it makes sense. They connect ideas in the text with what they already know. This is called *activation of prior knowledge.* As I work with a student, I remind myself that everything that he has seen, experienced, heard, felt, or tasted has a role in the interpretation of text. When new ideas conflict with previously held information, good readers make additions, subtractions, or revisions to the old information.

Additionally, good readers demonstrate the ability to identify and utilize the following elements:

- **main idea:** the central message of the passage,

- **supporting details:** statements used to promote the main idea,

- **clarifying devices:** methods and tools that the author uses to express thoughts,

- **drawing conclusions:** the ability to make accurate assessments based upon the material read,

- **inference:** the ability to "read between the lines" to determine what the author is saying without having been expressly informed, and

- **vocabulary in context:** understanding the meaning of new words based upon the surrounding text.

Chapter Summary

As we have examined the components of reading, let us now examine the primary difficulties that prevent students from mastering decoding. These fall under two categories: dyslexia and central processing disorder. A brief overview of each and some red flags to watch out for will be provided in Chapter 2.

chapter 2

Reading Difficulties

THERE are three main learning disorders that may be diagnosed in childhood: those related to reading, writing, and math (American Psychiatric Association, 2000). It is estimated that 80% of children with learning disorders have reading problems, making reading disabilities the most common form of learning disabilities (LDOnline, 2010). Most reading difficulties fall under two labels: dyslexia and central auditory processing disorder.

Dyslexia

Dyslexia is a common disorder that hinders the development of reading skills. Some researchers refer to dyslexia as a visual processing disorder that is neurological in nature. Dyslexia is defined by the International Dyslexia Association (2008) as

> . . . a specific learning disability that is neurological in origin.
> It is characterized by difficulties with accurate and/or fluent
> word recognition and by poor spelling and decoding abilities.
> These difficulties typically result from a deficit in the pho-
> nological component of language that is often unexpected
> in relation to other cognitive abilities and the provision of
> effective classroom instruction. Secondary consequences may
> include problems in reading comprehension and reduced read-
> ing experience that can impede the growth of vocabulary and
> background knowledge. (para. 1)

Students with dyslexia often struggle with language acquisition skills
despite having been exposed to scientific-based reading teaching
methodologies.

The visual pathway is the most important pathway involved with
the acquisition of written language skills; however, when discussing
visual processing ability, the actual process of seeing is not the issue.
There are two components to visual processing ability. The first involves
recognizing that words are a systematic string of individual graphemes
(letters). Each individual sequential combination represents a different
word. Therefore, students must be able to accurately track (from left to
right and top to bottom) and string together the individual phonemes
to produce words (called *word identification*). The second component
involves the acquisition of a visual image in the mind's eye based upon
the text decoded (called *concept imagery*). Visual processing ability is
believed to be determined by the level of functioning of the angular
gyrus, an area in the left hemisphere, which is the hemisphere that
serves as the language center of the human brain for 90% of the human
population. The angular gyrus sits on the junction of the temporal lobe
and the parietal lobe (see Figure 4), and it translates visual input into
auditory code. It is located directly behind Wernicke's area, the language center of the brain that is responsible for processing sound into
understandable words. The level of functioning of the angular gyrus
directly impacts the recognition and recall of words. Those students
who have a high level of angular gyrus activity have good visual memory. Those who have low levels of angular gyrus activity struggle with

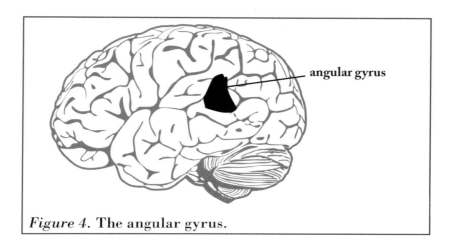

Figure 4. The angular gyrus.

reading, spelling, and composition due to a deficit in visual processing ability. These students have poor visual imagery and pronounced word recognition difficulty. Those toward the lower end of the spectrum, approximately 15%–20% of the world's population, can be described as having dyslexia with a specific visual processing difficulty (Learning Inside-Out, n.d.).

Visual imagery and word recognition ability have no direct correlation to a student's intelligence. Cultural icons such as Thomas Edison and Albert Einstein had visual imagery and word recognition skills toward the lowest end of the spectrum. In fact, both are thought to have had dyslexia.

Genetic Cause of Dyslexia

Researchers have known for quite some time that there is a genetic link between students with dyslexia and their families. Anecdotally, for each student with dyslexia with whom I have worked, either a parent or a grandparent recalled displaying symptoms of dyslexia during their academic careers. Researchers, however, have recently identified a connection between dyslexia and one gene in particular.

In November of 2005, Dr. Jeffrey Gruen, an associate professor at Yale School of Medicine, and his research team discovered that reading ability is influenced by a gene called DCDC2 (May, 2006). This gene is located on chromosome 6. The team studied 153 families of children with dyslexia and identified an altered stretch of DNA within the DCDC2 gene of the study group that correlated to a severe reading disability (May, 2006).

Dyslexia Red Flags

The following are common indicators of a language-based learning disability founded upon the visual processing of language (i.e., dyslexia):

- reversals of letters and words when learning to read;
- difficulty in direction and laterality;
- continued uncertainty of left- and righthandedness;
- uneven levels in academic achievement in various testing situations;
- persistent, unusual spelling errors;
- difficulty with mathematical skills;
- normal intelligence with patchy defects;
- slow and labored rate of reading;
- tendency to make wild guesses with new words;
- tendency to skip over small words (e.g., "a," "an," "the") while reading;
- tendency to mix up the order of letters;
- listening comprehension that is much better than reading comprehension;
- difficulty segmenting and blending individual letter sounds and syllables;
- a tough time learning to write one's own name;
- difficulty with sound/symbol correspondence;

- significant difficulty reading and spelling multisyllabic/longer words;

- difficulty recognizing and producing rhymes;

- confusion with letters that look alike (e.g., b/d/p, w/m, h/n, f/t);

- reduced awareness of word structure (i.e., prefix, roots, suffixes);

- difficulty with spelling and written composition;

- difficulty learning new information from text because of word reading errors;

- trouble learning a foreign language;

- significant difficulty with writing due to spelling and organization problems;

- reading and spelling errors that indicate difficulty sequencing sounds (e.g., "blast" vs. "blats");

- avoidance when asked to read aloud;

- omission of grammatical endings when reading and writing (e.g., "-s," "-ed," "-ing"); and

- difficulty remembering spelling of words over time.

The aforementioned list is not all inclusive. However, if a student demonstrates multiple indicators, parents and teachers are encouraged to pursue diagnostic testing from a qualified educational diagnostician to determine the presence of a specific language disability.

Auditory Processing Disorder

As visual processing ability referred to word recognition and recall of words after the image has been received by the eyes, auditory processing ability refers to what happens to impulses of sound in the brain after the ears have received them. Sound is processed into understandable words in an area of the temporal lobe of the dominant hemisphere called Wernicke's area (see Figure 5). The level of functioning of Wernicke's area directly impacts the auditory recognition and recall of words. Those students who have a high level of activity in Wernicke's area have good auditory processing ability. Those who have low levels of activity in this region struggle with the verbal skills associated with spoken words and ideas. These students have Auditory Processing Disorder (or Central Auditory Processing Disorder), a neurological condition that prevents students from being able to process information that they hear in the same way as other students without the disorder. Something interferes with the brain and its recognition and interpretation of auditory input, most notably the sounds composing speech. As a result, these students have difficulty remembering what was said (following oral directions), are highly susceptible to distracting noises, and find it extremely difficult to master foreign languages. As with visual imagery and word recognition and recall, auditory processing ability is independent of intelligence. Further, it has been suggested that 6 out of 10 people with visual processing difficulties also have auditory processing deficits (Myomancy, 2005).

Central Auditory Processing Disorder Red Flags

The following are common indicators of a language-based learning disability founded upon the auditory processing of language (i.e., central auditory processing disorder):

- difficulty remembering or following directions;
- poor auditory discrimination;
- poor ability to retain information;
- difficulty in finding the right word when speaking;
- excessive yawning and sleepiness in class;
- better performance with oral testing;

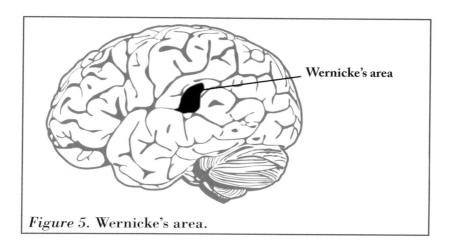

Figure 5. Wernicke's area.

- difficulty pronouncing words correctly (e.g., "aminal" for "animal");
- difficulty rhyming;
- problems learning the names of shapes and colors;
- difficulty learning letter names and letter sounds;
- difficulty understanding text because of underlying oral language problems;
- confusion with letters that have similar sounds (e.g., d/t, b/p, f/v);
- difficulty remembering common sight words (e.g., "was," "the," "and," "she"); and
- difficulty taking notes in class.

Again, if a student demonstrates multiple indicators, parents and teachers are encouraged to pursue diagnostic testing from a qualified educational diagnostician to determine the presence of a specific language disability.

How Are Reading Difficulties Addressed in School?

Students with diagnosed reading difficulties are typically provided with either an Individualized Education Program (IEP) or a 504 Plan in public schools, both of which are free of charge to families. The provision of these plans are based on federal law (the Individuals With Disabilities Education Improvement Act of 2004, or IDEA, and Section 504 of the Rehabilitation Act of 1973). Provision of the IEP requires diagnosis of a disability; the 504 Plan can be provided without specific diagnosis. Both contain accommodations and adjustments to the classroom environment and curriculum that should be made by the teaching staff. We'll concentrate on the IEP in this book.

The sole purpose of the IEP is to level the playing field and to help kids with special needs succeed in school. The IEP describes the goals set for a child during the school year by the IEP team, of which parents are a part, as well as any special support needed to help achieve them. Generally, the services and goals outlined in an IEP can be provided in a standard classroom setting. This can be done in the regular classroom or in a special resource room in the regular school designed for a group of students with similar needs who are brought together. In rare circumstances, students may need to be placed in a special school for students with specific learning disabilities. In these circumstances, the teachers in the school have special training (language instructors trained to teach children with dyslexia) to assist students with reading and spelling as it relates to their other academic endeavors. Although all efforts are made to ensure that each child stays within the regular classroom, situations do arise where special needs are best addressed in other environments, like resource classrooms, special schools, and tutoring.

How Students Are Referred

The referral process usually begins when someone associated with the student, typically a teacher or a parent, is concerned that the student may be experiencing academic difficulties. I wish to highlight that the parent may initiate the referral process. If you feel that your student is struggling academically, reach out to the school counselor or psychologist and request an assessment of your child's reading abilities. Several steps should be taken to gather information on the student's academic performance, including:

- a conference with parents and teachers of the student;

- a meeting with the student, parents, and counselor or psychologist;

- an observation of the student in and outside of an academic environment; and

- a thorough analysis of the student's complete academic performance.

All of the aforementioned steps are integral components in determining the causes of your student's academic struggles. After the collection of the data, the decision is made as to whether or not to move forward with educational diagnostics with a qualified diagnostician. It is important to note that regardless of what the school determines, you, as a parent, decide whether to have your child assessed. Note that children with disabilities who are placed in private elementary schools and secondary schools by their parents do not have the same rights as kids with disabilities who are enrolled in public schools. Private schools are not federally mandated to provide services.

For clarity, if the school does not independently pursue educational diagnostics without prompting, you may request it at the school district's expense. If you choose to do so, you'll be asked to sign a permission form that will detail who the diagnostician is that they have selected and the types of tests to be used. A complete battery of tests should include measures of specific school skills such as reading or math (e.g., Woodcock-Johnson III Normative Update Complete) and tests of cognitive development and abilities (e.g., Wechsler's Intelligence Scales for Children—Fourth Edition). If warranted, parents may wish to incorporate tests that cover specific speech and language skills. (Note that many schools use specific tests purchased by the district, and parents may not be able to recommend specific tests.) Testing does not necessarily mean that a child will receive services, neither does the presence of a diagnosed disability. To be eligible, the disability must affect a child's functioning at school.

To determine eligibility, a multidisciplinary team of professionals will evaluate the child based on educational diagnostics, observations, standardized tests, and classroom assessments and homework. For a thorough treatment of the IEP process and how it's conducted in schools, I recommend *Special Needs Advocacy Resource Book* by Rich Weinfeld and Michelle R. Davis.

Chapter Summary

The visual and auditory pathways play a crucial role in the acquisition of written and spoken language skills, and deficits in these two key areas require specialized intervention. Chapter 3 examines how these interventions may appear in the classroom and at home.

Strategies for the Classroom and Home to Remediate Reading Difficulties

I N addition to the more structured approach prescribed later in this book, there are general strategies that teachers and parents may utilize that will provide some relief to students who are struggling with the reading process. This chapter looks at a few of the general strategies that teachers and parents can implement to help their struggling readers.

Learning Styles

Many of the teachers in public education are unaware that different learning styles exist, or if they are aware of their existence, they are unprepared to teach in a way that accommodates the distinct learning style. Learning styles are simply different approaches or ways of learning. Better stated, learning styles are the methods through which the student learns best. Teachers can implement various strategies to help students learn in their preferred styles. In some cases, these strategies can help students overcome some of the weaknesses they face in having a reading difficulty. Parents can also become aware of their children's preferred learning styles and use them to help aid their children with homework and independent learning. A simple search for "learning styles inventory" online will garner multiple inventories, surveys, and observation forms teachers and parents can use to determine a student's learning style. We'll discuss three learning styles in this chapter: visual, auditory, and tactile-kinesthetic.

Visual Learners

Visual learners learn through seeing. These learners need to see the teacher's body language and facial expressions to fully understand the content of a lesson. These students tend to prefer sitting at the front of the classroom to avoid visual obstructions. They frequently think in pictures and learn best from visual displays including diagrams, illustrated textbooks, overhead transparencies, videos, and handouts. During a lecture, visual learners prefer to either take detailed notes to absorb the information or receive a printed copy of the instructor's lecture notes. Visual learners are "big picture" people, and, as such, make great navigators, artists, inventors, architects, mechanics, and engineers.

The study habits of visual learners are strongest if they involve a quiet location where the student can view notes and materials. It is imperative that these students limit their visual distractions as they scan pertinent chapters and use diagrams to reinforce sequencing.

Auditory Learners

Auditory learners learn through listening. They learn best through verbal discussions, lectures, and dialogue. Auditory learners may ask frequent questions in order to clarify information as they interpret the underlying meanings of speech through listening to tone of voice, pitch, and cadence. Information in written form may have little meaning for the auditory learner until it is heard. These learners benefit from reading text aloud and using a tape recorder, as they think in words instead of pictures. Auditory learners are wonderful speakers, and they are very persuasive. With this skill set, auditory learners make great journalists, writers, lawyers, and politicians.

When studying, auditory learners also benefit from having a quiet location where they can view notes and materials. Here, though, it is imperative that these students limit their auditory distractions as they read their notes aloud. Auditory learners should never study while listening to music. Further, these learners will greatly benefit from having a partner who will ask questions, forcing the auditory learner to verbalize the information coherently.

Tactile-Kinesthetic Learners

Tactile-kinesthetic learners learn through moving, doing, and touching. They learn best through a hands-on approach, as they need to actively explore the world around them. They may find it hard to sit still for long periods of time and may become distracted by their need for activity and exploration. These learners use their bodies to solve problems and express themselves through movement. As such, tactile-kinesthetic learners make great athletes, dancers, and actors.

When studying, tactile-kinesthetic learners benefit from having a quiet location where the student can view notes and materials. This is where the similarities in study habits with auditory and visual learners end. In order for tactile-kinesthetic learners to embrace academic material, a fine motor neurological gateway must be introduced. The cleanest method in which to activate the neurological pathway for muscle movement is to make sure that students are physically comfortable, and have them write, write, write. If they speak what they are writing, the tract of articulation adds an additional tactile enforcement as the muscles of the tongue and jaw are activated.

How Different Learning Styles May Manifest

Based upon individual learning preferences, humans respond to external stimuli in different forms. Given the same circumstances, a visual learner will respond differently than an auditory learner, who will respond differently than a tactile-kinesthetic learner. View the following situations and how different learning styles will manifest themselves in identical situations. Teachers can use these as prompts for helping their students with reading difficulties adjust the way they study and learn.

- When studying for a test . . .

  - A visual learner will read notes, read headings in a book, and look at diagrams and illustrations.

  - An auditory learner will have someone ask him questions or repeat facts (silently[2] or aloud) to himself.

  - A tactile-kinesthetic learner will write things out on index cards and make models.

- When listening to music . . .

  - A visual learner will daydream (see things that go with the music).

  - An auditory learner will hum/sing along.

  - A tactile-kinesthetic learner will move with the music, such as by tapping her foot.

- When solving a problem . . .

  - A visual learner will make a list, organize the steps, and check them off as he is done.

  - An auditory learner will make a few phone calls and talk to friends or experts.

2   Even while reading silently, we "hear" a voice in our heads that must be processed by Wernicke's area, the area in the language hemisphere that turns sound into understandable speech.

○ A tactile-kinesthetic learner will make a model of the problem.

• When learning how a computer works . . .

○ A visual learner will watch a movie/read a book about it.

○ An auditory learner will listen to someone explain it.

○ A tactile-kinesthetic learner will take the computer apart and try to figure it out for herself.

• When entering a museum . . .

○ A visual learner will find a map showing the locations of the various exhibits.

○ An auditory learner will talk to a museum guide and ask about exhibits.

○ A tactile-kinesthetic learner will go into the first exhibit that looks interesting and read directions later.

• When dining out, the meal would be ruined for . . .

○ a visual learner if the lights were too bright.

○ an auditory learner if the music was too loud.

○ a tactile-kinesthetic learner if the chairs were uncomfortable.

• If you were at a party, what would you be most likely to remember the next day?

○ For a visual learner, it would be the faces of the people there, but not the names.

○ For an auditory learner, it would be the names, but not the faces.

    ○   For a tactile-kinesthetic learner, it would be the things he did and said while he was there.

  •   What is most distracting for you when you are trying to concentrate?

    ○   For a visual learner, it would be visual distractions.

    ○   For an auditory learner, it would be other noises.

    ○   For a tactile-kinesthetic learner, it would be other sensations, like hunger, tight shoes, or worry.

With the current structure of the public schools, little time is available for the accommodation of all three learning styles in the mainstream classroom setting. Most educational delivery caters to the visual learner alone. Imagine the difficulties faced by an auditory learner in a class of 30 who must frequently ask questions for clarification in order to thoroughly understand the presented material. Further, imagine the difficulties faced by a tactile-kinesthetic learner who experiences difficulty sitting for an extended period. Resultantly, this type of learner feels an overwhelming impulse to stand, move, and touch things. Anyone familiar with the procedures of public educational institutions understands that these types of students would be quickly labeled as "problem" children and most likely would be placed in either disciplinary situations or special education classes. Controversially, testing for the preferred learning styles of minority public school children is seldom, if ever, undertaken.

What teachers can do is carefully observe their students for the signs of the learning styles mentioned in this chapter. When you discover that a student with reading difficulties is also an auditory learner, adjust his or her assignments to allow the student to listen to a lengthy class novel as an audiobook. Tactile-kinesthetic learners might be given the option to practice writing letters with a large, individual chalkboard or dry erase board. Visual learners might be allowed to present their research findings in a diagram or large chart instead of in essay form. There are multiple ways teachers can implement learning styles that are beyond the scope of this book, but it is definitely encouraged that they pay attention to the learning styles of the struggling readers in their classrooms and see if adjustments can be made to aid them with their difficulties.

Assistive Technology

Assistive technology is defined as any item, piece of equipment, or product system, whether acquired commercially off the shelf, modified, or customized, that is used to increase, maintain, or improve the functional capabilities of children with disabilities; however, the term does not include a medical device that is surgically implanted (Individuals with Disabilities Education Improvement Act of 2004). Essentially, these devices are used to remediate and/or compensate for deficits in the five critical areas of effective reading instruction: phonological awareness, phonics, fluency, vocabulary, and comprehension.

Parents and teachers should consider the use of assistive technology because the components serve to compensate for deficits in the aforementioned areas by providing tangible solutions and assistance that allow students to successfully complete academic tasks. These devices typically fall into the following categories:

- positioning aids,
- tracking aids,
- contrast aids,
- word identification aids,
- books in alternate format, and
- reading software.

Teachers should be able to access assistive technology to help struggling readers in their classrooms by contacting their school's assistive technology specialist or special education department chairperson. Speech-language pathologists and occupational therapists on your campus may have some of these devices to lend to you as well. Parents can often purchase assistive technology online from sites like http://DonJohnston.com; be warned, however, that products can get costly. In some cases, children with documented reading disabilities and an Individualized Education Program (IEP) will be given access to these tools to use both at home and at school.

Positioning Aids

Positioning aids allow for the most beneficial positioning of text, making the content more visible to students with reading difficulties. The most common positioning aid is one that places the book at a slant. For some students with reading visual processing deficits, reading books at a vertical slant aids in tracking, sequencing, and, resultantly, word recognition. The slanted work surface presents all text characters at the same perspective. Book stands that change the position of texts can be purchased commercially, or teachers and parents can create their own. Many of the stands also offer some kind of band, peg, or page holder to allow for hands-free use. A great resource for finding positioning aids and learning more about them is the Georgia Project for Assistive Technology site at http://www.gpat.org/Georgia-Project-for-Assistive-Technology/Pages/Positioning-Aids.aspx.

Tracking Aids

Tracking aids enable students with visual tracking difficulties to maintain their place in the text. The best tracking aid happens to be the most inexpensive one. I recommend that students use an index card. The technique involves the student placing the index card directly *above* the line that they are reading. The card must be directly above the line because, in the English code, we read from top to bottom and from left to right. We want the eyes of the student to swing freely from the end of the line (on the right) to the beginning of the line beneath it (on the left). Having the card above the line being read prevents the tracking aid from being an obstruction to this process. More about using index cards in this way can be found in Chapter 6. Some schools may have other tracking aids they have already purchased for use by children with reading difficulties, such as reading windows or transparencies. Again, the Georgia Project for Assistive Technology (see http://www.gpat.org/Georgia-Project-for-Assistive-Technology/Pages/Tracking-Aids.aspx) is a great resource for learning more about and finding tracking aids if a parent or teacher chooses not to use an index card.

Contrast Aids

Contrast aids promote visual acuity with text by contrasting the foreground-background relationship. The Georgia Project for Assistive Technology (n.d.) noted that contrast aids can help students who have difficulty reading text due to visual discomfort. Often, these students report that the text is fuzzy or exhibit fatigue, displayed as rubbing their eyes or fidgeting when reading. Again, the best contrast aid happens to be the most inexpensive one. I recommend that students use a florescent yellow highlighter. Students can highlight key words or concepts found in the text or thesis statements as part of the construction of a prereading map (see p. 40 for more on making these maps with students). Other contrast aids that might be found in schools include overlays or filters, colored lights, and highlighter tape. Parents and teachers can also adjust the background and font colors when using computer word processing programs. Resources and vendors for purchasing commercial contrast aids can be found at http://www.gpat.org/Georgia-Project-for-Assistive-Technology/Pages/Contrast-Aids.aspx.

Word Identification Aids

Word identification aids offer portable solutions for the decoding of multisyllabic words that present as problematic for students. The tools, including portable electronic dictionaries and pens, are designed to be utilized when the parent is not around. Some of the most popular devices are the Franklin Electronic Dictionary and Franklin Electronic speller tools. Several different versions of these electronic tools exist, and most can be purchased from standard retailers like Amazon.com or Best Buy. I would be remiss, however, if I did not mention that physical dictionaries offer excellent opportunities for mastering the decoding and pronunciation of multisyllabic words. After each entry in the dictionary, parents will find a pronunciation guide for the word. Many dictionaries can also be found online, and several dictionary applications exist for download and use on students' iPads, smart phones, eReaders, and other devices.

Books in Alternate Format

Books in alternate format are literally those that present the printed text in formats more compatible with struggling readers. The alternative format that I highly recommend is an audiobook. The audiobook presents text in auditory format that will allow students to follow along as the text is read. A wonderful source for a large selection of audiobooks is Learning Ally (http://www.learningally.org; formally known as Recording for the Blind and Dyslexic). In addition, audiobooks may be ordered commercially through Amazon.com, the Barnes and Noble website (http://www.BN.com), and other online retailers.

Another option is the eBook, which can come in many different formats. These can be PDFs of books or specially formatted books for various electronic readers. Popular eReaders include the Amazon Kindle, the Barnes and Noble nook, and the iPad. Most popular fiction and nonfiction titles, including picture books and those often taught in schools, can be found for purchase and download on these devices. In addition, many public libraries now offer the option of checking out eBooks and downloading them for a specified period of time on either a personal device or a library-issued eReader. The eReaders on the market all offer a variety of options for accommodating various reading needs, such as enlarging or changing fonts, highlighting passages, marking pages and words, built-in dictionaries, and text-to-speech software, which reads the words on the screen aloud for students.

Reading Software

Reading software is designed to provide scaffolding to the struggling reader. Often referred to as text-to-speech software, the software reads the text for the student, typically highlighting the text as it reads, thus assisting students with tracking issues. The most valuable reading software happens to be the most expensive: Kurzweil 3000 (see http://www.kurzweiledu.com/products.html for more information). With this reading software, the pitch and cadence of the voice is adjustable, as well as the gender of the voice. The cost of Kurzweil 3000 is approximately $1,500, but it is a worthwhile investment. In addition to reading and highlighting the text, the software allows students to input definitions for unknown words directly into the text. Some schools will have access to Kurzweil already, so teachers are encouraged to check with their district's assistive technology specialist or special education department first. Other less expensive text-to-speech options do exist for parents to use at home, including some built into computer operating systems or eReaders.

Prereading Maps

To explain the concept of a prereading map, I like to use the analogy of driving to Chicago from anywhere in Florida. In order for the analogy to be effective, you have to remember the days before global positioning systems (GPS). Of course today, we can just get in the car and plug our destination into the trusty GPS and off we go. Before GPS, in order to take a road trip where we did not know the route, we would never just hop in the car and start driving without a clue to where we were going. We needed a map at the very least. We needed something to explain what was coming, what to look for, where to turn, what highway to get on and get off, and where to find certain key elements. Well, students who struggle with reading difficulties when they approach most reading assignments are like the old drivers who just hop in the car and start driving without a clue about where they are going. To aid students with difficulties in word identification and/or concept imagery, I recommend the creation of prereading maps.

A prereading map is a simple map of what is coming in the text, what to look for, and where to find certain key information. The map is not a challenge to create, because its creation is based solely upon the knowledge of the structure of the paragraph. One thing that readers should understand is that the paragraph is governed by rules. By definition, all writers who use these paragraphs are governed by the same rules. Once readers know what the rules are, there should be fewer surprises found within the text as readers progress through the written materials. Additionally, once we have our maps created, students will have a much easier time finding information in the text for review or exam preparation.

The Paragraph

A paragraph is a collection of related sentences dealing with a single topic. This is the most basic rule in the construction of a paragraph. If the author begins to transition to a new concept or idea, it belongs in a new paragraph. This is information that struggling readers can use to their advantage as they construct a map of what the author is presenting and the order of the information that is supplied in the text. Plus, we know that in formal academic writing such as the type found in textbooks, each paragraph must have three key components: a topic sentence, supporting details, and a conclusion. Again, this is information that struggling readers can use to their advantage.

The topic sentence. A topic sentence is a sentence that indicates to the reader what idea the paragraph is going to cover. In terms of our prereading map, the topic sentence becomes a critical component toward the construction of a guide to what is coming in the text. Here, there are two caveats, though. First, not all paragraphs have topic sentences that are clearly defined, and second, topic sentences can occur anywhere in the paragraph. For most writers, for all intents and purposes, the topic sentence appears sooner rather than later in the paragraph. Let's look at one paragraph:

> **The ideal form of instruction would be one where the student feels a sense of empowerment over the learning process.** There are many roads that may lead to the development of the sense of educational empowerment. The key is to create an educationally conducive environment that provides opportunity for the fostering of emotional stability. As the development of decision-making skills lies at the root of the ideal educational process, the ideal form of instruction must provide a safe, comfortable environment for the students to practice and strengthen these skills. Students must be willing to make choices and accept the consequences in order to assume a role as a maturing adult in American society. As adults, we are well aware that sometimes, the consequences of our actions are good. Sometimes, they are bad. It is the role of educational institutions to provide an environment where students feel safe to try.

Clearly, the entire paragraph above discusses the ideal form of instruction and its affirmative impact on the development of a student. Therefore, in the above paragraph, the topic sentence is the first sentence in the paragraph. Such is not the case in the next paragraph:

> The College Board reported that the average score for women bound for college is 43 points below the average score for men. **The greatest disparities, however, have been documented between African-Americans and Whites.** African-Americans score lower than Whites on vocabulary, reading, and math tests, as well as on tests such as the SAT. This gap appears before kindergarten and persists into adulthood. The average African-American student scores below 70%–80% of the White students of the same age. Similar issues arise when Mexican American and Latino students, as well as

Native American students, are compared to White students, although this phenomenon has not been studied as widely. Among seniors who entered college in the fall of 1999, African-Americans' average scores on the SAT I Verbal were 93 points below White students' average scores.

Even though the paragraph above mentions the disparities between college-bound women and college-bound men, the real purpose of the paragraph is to discuss the disparities between African-American students and White students. We know this based upon the remaining sentences in the paragraph, the supporting details, and the concluding sentence. Therefore, the topic sentence is the second sentence in the paragraph.

Supporting details. Supporting details (or supporting sentences) usually appear after the topic sentence. (In situations where the topic sentence appears later in the paragraph, supporting details can entice or lead up to the topic sentence.) They come after the topic sentence and provide details that develop and support the main idea. Readers can easily identify the number of supporting sentences within a paragraph. Because we know that one sentence must be the topic sentence, and one sentence must be the concluding sentence, the remaining sentences in the paragraph are typically supporting sentences. For example, in a paragraph with six sentences, four of the sentences will be those that support the main idea of the paragraph. If we look at the first paragraph again, we find that of the nine sentences in the paragraph, we know that the first sentence is our topic sentence. The next seven sentences provide details that develop and support the main idea or topic sentence

The ideal form of instruction would be one where the student feels a sense of empowerment over the learning process. **There are many roads that may lead to the development of the sense of educational empowerment. The key is to create an educationally conducive environment that provides opportunity for the fostering of emotional stability. As the development of decision-making skills lies at the root of**

the ideal educational process, the ideal form of instruction must provide a safe, comfortable environment for the students to practice and strengthen these skills. Students must be willing to make choices and accept the consequences in order to assume a role as a maturing adult in American society. As adults, we are well aware that sometimes, the consequences of our actions are good. Sometimes, they are bad. It is the role of educational institutions to provide an environment where students feel safe to try.

We have a similar situation if we reexamine the second paragraph:

The College Board reported that the average score for women bound for college is 43 points below the average score for men. The greatest disparities, however, have been documented between African-Americans and Whites. **African-Americans score lower than Whites on vocabulary, reading, and math tests, as well as on tests such as the SAT. This gap appears before kindergarten and persists into adulthood. The average African-American student scores below 70%–80% of the White students of the same age. Similar issues arise when Mexican American and Latino students, as well as Native American students, are compared to White students, although this phenomenon has not been studied as widely.** Among seniors who entered college in the fall of 1999, African-Americans' average scores on the SAT I Verbal were 93 points below White students' average scores.

In our reexamination of the second paragraph, we find that of the seven sentences in the paragraph, we know that the second sentence is our topic sentence. The next four sentences provide details that develop and support the main idea or topic sentence.

The conclusion. The conclusion (also known as a closing sentence) is the last sentence in a paragraph. It restates the main idea of the paragraph using different words and frequently sums up the paragraph in preparation for a change in topics. Although the wording may be different, the underlying meaning is the same as that of the topic sentence.

In our reexamination of the first paragraph, we find that the concluding sentence restates our topic sentence using different words and sums up the paragraph so that the topic can be changed:

> The ideal form of instruction would be one where the student feels a sense of empowerment over the learning process. There are many roads that may lead to the development of the sense of educational empowerment. The key is to create an educationally conducive environment that provides opportunity for the fostering of emotional stability. As the development of decision-making skills lies at the root of the ideal educational process, the ideal form of instruction must provide a safe, comfortable environment for the students to practice and strengthen these skills. Students must be willing to make choices and accept the consequences in order to assume a role as a maturing adult in American society. As adults, we are well aware that sometimes, the consequences of our actions are good. Sometimes, they are bad. **It is the role of educational institutions to provide an environment where students feel safe to try.**

Constructing the Prereading Map

Now that we understand the formation of the paragraph, we can use this information to accurately map the layout of the text that we are going to read. Our first task is to identify the topic sentence. Once we have the topic sentence identified, we sum up the topic of the paragraph and write it off to the side. Look at the following example:

Standardized tests fail to understand that each of our children is an individual entity. Each child has a unique set of fingerprints. Each has a unique vocal pitch, tone, and cadence. Each has a unique retinal scan and a unique body chemistry. If modern science accepts the aforementioned as true, one may be puzzled as to why so many within the realm of education expect all of our children to learn in the same way.

Each child is different ·

In this paragraph, we have identified our topic sentence as the first sentence in the paragraph. After a cursory glance at the remaining sentences, we now know that the entire paragraph discusses how each child is different. We then write "Each child is different" off to the side of the paragraph and move on to the next paragraph, shown below:

Many of today's colleges and universities have prepared and continue to prepare teacher candidates as if their future students were computers produced on the same assembly line, carrying the same software. Merely download the information, click on the icon that appears on your desktop, and run the program. **Rarely considered are the students who learn differently due to the fact that they have different "software."** When the student who learns differently does not respond well to the mainstream instruction method, the educational system applies stigmas such as "slow" or "lazy." Yet, in the dawn of educational shortsightedness, a few key educational leaders have had the insight that, as there is more than one type of individual, there must be more than one type of human intelligence. If there is more than one type of human intelligence, it follows that there must be more than one type of instruction.

Some students learn differently ·

Again, we have identified our topic sentence. Here, it is not the first sentence or even the second, but the third sentence in the paragraph. After a cursory glance at the remaining sentences, we now know that the entire paragraph discusses how some students learn differently than others. We then write "Some students learn differently" off to the side of the paragraph and move on to the next.

Using this simple procedure for each paragraph in the reading assignment, you can create a tool that allows students to quickly surmise how the author has constructed the text before reading for comprehension. The chances of getting lost are greatly reduced once students have a prereading map. Additionally, when it comes time for review or exam preparation, students now know exactly where to look in order to locate certain information. Creating their own prereading maps is a great exercise for students to undergo before they start their reading assignments.

Picture Tasks

Picture tasks are a wonderful tool to foster reading comprehension skills. These tasks encourage struggling readers to think cognitively about what they see, process the information within the realm of what the student has previously experienced, and infer and make abstract connections—tasks that must be used for good reading comprehension. Parents and teachers must realize that good readers bring all that they know and have experienced to the process of concept imagery (pulling meaning from print). Through the use of picture tasks, students are asked to activate all prior learning in order to make determinations as they answer questions of who, what, where, when, and why. The key as they are answering questions is to remember that we are trying to activate their prior knowledge. All answers are legitimate except "I don't know."

Let's demonstrate the activity using Figure 6, a photo that my wife and I took in Montreal during our honeymoon 5 years ago. It's a photo of our carriage driver and his horse. There is nothing special going on in the photo, which is precisely the point. You may use any image that you feel is acceptable. These images may be found in photo albums, magazines, newspapers, online, or in your personal collec-

Figure 6. Image for picture task.

tion. Nevertheless, let's get back to the photo. The dialogue between you and the student is designed to engage the student in conversation, encouraging him to bring all of his life experience to the comprehension of the activity that is taking place in the image. The dialogue based upon Figure 6 with an elementary or middle school student may go something like the following. Please note the logical connections that may be made:

> **You:** Let's talk about this picture. What do you see in the picture?
>
> **Student:** I see a man and a horse. I see people in the back sitting on steps. Other people in the back are standing up. I also see a car behind the horse.
>
> **You:** Okay. Let's talk about the man. Tell me about him.
>
> **Student:** He has long hair, and he is wearing a cowboy hat.
>
> **You:** Why is he wearing a cowboy hat?

Student: Because he's a cowboy.

You: What makes you think that he's a cowboy?

Student: Because he's wearing a cowboy hat and standing next to his horse.

You: Let's talk about the horse. What can you tell me about the horse?

Student: It's a big horse.

You: Yes, it's big. What else can you tell me about the horse?

Student: It's brown and has light-colored hair. And it's wearing a bunch of stuff.

You: Yes, it's wearing some things. Why do you think that it is wearing those things?

Student: Those are things that the cowboy needs. They used horses to carry their stuff.

You: Okay. Let's talk about the people in the back. You said that some are on the steps.

Student: They're sitting on the steps watching the cowboy and his horse.

You: Why are they watching the cowboy and his horse?

Student: Because they're at a rodeo, and he's doing tricks.

You: Is he very good at doing tricks?

Student: Well, not many people are watching him.

You: What does that tell you?

Student: If he was good, there would be more people watching him. Some of the people who are standing back there aren't even looking.

You: Where does this take place?

Again, this is just a sample of a dialogue based upon Figure 6 with an elementary or middle school student. The dialogue may proceed in whichever direction you choose. Please keep in mind that the purpose of the dialogue between you and the student is designed to engage the student in conversation, encouraging her to bring all of her life experiences to the comprehension of the activity that is taking place in the image. These types of conversations are easily transferrable to class reading activities such as guided reading or group story time.

Sight Words and The Dolch Word List

The Dolch Word List, a list of English (mostly Anglo-Saxon) sight words, was compiled by Dr. Edward William Dolch in 1948. Dr. Dolch compiled the list based on words used in children's books in the 1930s and 1940s. The list contains 220 words (see Table 1 for a full list of the Dolch words). These words are called "sight words" because many of the 220 Dolch words are nonphonetic, meaning that the words are not pronounced the way that they are seen nor are they spelled the way that they are spoken. Students must not only quickly recognize the word "on sight" in order to achieve reading fluency, but students must also be able to spell the words from memory. Because these sight words make up more than 50% of any general text, teaching the Dolch words lays the foundation for reading skills in the English code. Almost 100% of the words that students will encounter from prekindergarten through the third grade are based upon Anglo-Saxon word construction including sight words.

There are multiple strategies for teaching sight words to students. Some resources suggest that one-on-one practice with adults in learning sight words increase the chances of a child adding a sight word to his long-term memory (K12Reader, n.d.). Parents and teachers can help students learn sight words through simple strategies like flashcards, posters, illustrations, word walls, sentence strips, and games. Repetition of the words and hearing the words aloud or within the context they are to be used can also aid students in remembering these words. For more detailed ideas on teaching the sight words, parents and teachers can check out the following website: http://www.

Table 1

Dolch Sight Word Lists

Pre-Primer	a	`and	away	big	blue	can	come
	down	find	for	funny	go	help	here
	I	in	is	it	jump	little	look
	make	me	my	not	one	play	red
	run	said	see	the	three	to	two
	up	we	where	yellow	you		
Primer	all	am	are	at	ate	be	black
	brown	but	came	did	do	eat	four
	get	good	have	he	into	like	must
	new	no	now	on	our	out	so
	please	pretty	ran	ride	saw	say	she
	soon	that	there	they	this	too	under
	want	was	well	went	what	white	who
	will	with	yes				
First Grade	after	again	an	any	ask	as	by
	could	every	fly	from	give	going	had
	has	her	him	his	how	just	know
	let	live	may	of	old	once	open
	over	put	round	some	stop	take	thank
	them	then	think	walk	were	where	
Second Grade	always	around	because	been	before	best	both
	buy	call	cold	does	don't	fast	first
	five	found	gave	goes	green	its	made
	many	off	or	pull	read	right	sing
	sit	sleep	tell	their	these	those	upon
	us	use	very	wash	which	why	wish
	work	would	write	your			
Third Grade	about	better	bring	carry	clean	cut	done
	draw	drink	eight	fall	far	full	got
	grow	hold	hot	hurt	if	keep	kind
	laugh	light	long	much	myself	never	only
	own	pick	seven	shall	show	six	small
	start	ten	today	together	try	warm	

k12reader.com/sight-word-teaching-strategies. In addition, a simple search for "Dolch sight words" online pulls up many, many resources for teaching these words, including online games and some commercial products (although with the list included in this book, it should be easy for parents and teachers to create their own products). Often, teaching students the sight words can help them remediate many of their struggles with vocabulary, allowing them to move on to more difficult reading materials and vocabulary study.

Phonemic Awareness Drills

As discussed in Chapter 1, phonemic awareness is the awareness that words are composed of sequences or strings of individual sounds called phonemes. To be independent readers, students must have the ability to identify and visually imagine the number, order, and identity of sounds and letters within words. These abilities underlie accurate word attack, word recognition, reading fluency, and spelling. Children who have phonemic awareness skills are likely to have an easier time learning to read and spell than children who have few or none of these skills. Children with weakness in these functions add, omit, substitute, and reverse sounds and letters within words while reading and spelling.

Again, the five key skills that serve as the foundation of phonemic awareness are:

- **phoneme replication:** the ability to repeat a sound heard;

- **blending:** the ability to join a string of phonemes together to create a word;

- **segmenting:** the ability to break a word into its individual phonemes;

- **substitution/deletion:** the ability to replace a phoneme with a new phoneme or to remove a phoneme altogether, creating a new word; and

- **rhyming:** the ability to find words with the same rhyme.

Phoneme replication is relatively easy to drill (in my structured approach in Chapter 6, each language arts/language training session begins with a phonics deck that takes care of this; therefore, I suggest that teachers and parents check out the section of that chapter on the phonics deck for more information on how to do this). The four remaining skills, however, require more dedicated exercises, such as the ones below.

Segmenting and Rhyming

Teachers and parents can use scripts to help students learn to segment words and find rhymes for words and sounds. I've included a few sample scripts in Figure 7, but more can be found in Appendix A. After teaching students about syllables, consonant digraphs, blends, and clusters (see Chapter 4), sit down with a struggling reader and a few scripts. Go through the scripts slowly, using the given parent instructions. Make sure that the students' answers match those included in the script (although there is flexibility in the section on rhymes). Scripts that the students get correct can go in one pile; incorrect ones can go in another pile. Then, incorrect scripts can be reviewed again until they can be moved into the stack of correct responses. Teachers and parents can use this template to make additional scripts for reviewing vocabulary words when needed.

Blending

One way to teach blending to students is through simple drills, showing the students the sounds in order and asking them to blend them together into single words. An example list that can be used in blending drills can be found in Figure 8. Simply place the phonemes on a card or chart and have the students attempt to blend them into words. Incorrect blends can be reviewed further with the students until they have mastered the various sounds.

Teacher/Parent Instruction	Expected Student Answers
Say "slime."	"slime"
Sound it out for me.	/ s / / l / / ī / / m /
How many sounds are in the word "slime"?	Four
How many syllables?	One
How many digraphs?	Zero
How many blends?	One
How many clusters?	Zero
Give me five words that rhyme with "slime."	lime, dime, chime, mime, prime

Teacher/Parent Instruction	Expected Student Answers
Say "chat."	"chat"
Sound it out for me.	/ ch / / ă / / t /
How many sounds are in the word "chat"?	Three
How many syllables?	One
How many digraphs?	One
How many blends?	Zero
How many clusters?	Zero
Give me five words that rhyme with "chat."	bat, cat, fat, mat, rat

Teacher/Parent Instruction	Expected Student Answers
Say "jump."	"jump"
Sound it out for me.	/ j / / ŭ / / m / / p /
How many sounds are in the word "jump"?	Four
How many syllables?	One
How many digraphs?	Zero
How many blends?	One
How many clusters?	Zero
Give me five words that rhyme with "jump."	hump, bump, lump, trump, grump

Figure 7. Sample scripts for segmenting and rhyming practice.

Have the students blend the following sounds to make a word:			
/ s / / l / / ă / / m /	slam	/ f / / ĭ / / s / / t /	fist
/ f / / ĭ / / t /	fit	/ b / / ĕ / / d / / z /	beds
/ b / / ŭ / / m / / p /	bump	/ l / / ŭ / / k /	luck
/ s / / p / / ĭ / / l /	spill	/ t / / r / / ă / / sh /	trash
/ t / / r / / ă / / p /	trap	/ g / / ō / / s / / t /	ghost
/ m / / ā / / l /	mail	/ sh / / r / / ĕ / / d /	shred
/ s / / ŏ / / k / / s /	socks	/ d / / r / / ŭ / / m /	drum
/ s / / p / / r / / ĭ / / n / / t /	sprint	/ s / / t / / ŏ / / p /	stop
/ b / / ă / / g /	bag	/ s / / t / / ă / / n / / d /	stand
/ d / / ŏ / / k / / s /	docks	/ j / / ŏ / / b /	job
/ t / / r / / ŭ / / n / / k /	trunk	/ d / / r / / ĭ / / p /	drip
/ s / / l / / ĭ / / k /	slick	/ k / / ŭ / / p /	cup
/ k / / r / / ă / / m /	cram	/ f / / ĕ / / l / / t /	felt
/ b / / r / / ă / / s /	brass	/ b / / r / / ĭ / / k /	brick
/ d / / r / / ŏ / / p /	drop	/ s / / k / / ō / / l / / d /	scold
/ s / / l / / ŏ / / b /	slob	/ t / / ĕ / / m / / p / / t /	tempt
/ m / / ĕ / / n / / t /	meant	/ s / / t / / ŭ / / n /	stun
/ w / / ĕ / / s / / t /	west	/ t / / w / / ĭ / / n /	twin
/ d / / r / / ă / / b /	drab	/ s / / k / / r / / ā / / p /	scrape
/ m / / ŭ / / d /	mud	/ l / / ī / / t /	light

Figure 8. Blending drills list.

Phoneme Deletion and Substitution Drills

Phoneme deletion and substitution drills simply ask students to take one letter or sound from a word and replace it with a different letter or sound. By doing so, the students learn to create and understand new words. Figure 9 has a sample of one simple phoneme deletion and substitution drill that both parents and teachers can practice with students easily. A fuller list of these drills can be found in Appendix B.

Ask students to make the directed alterations to the following words:

Say "drag."
    Change the last sound to / b /.   drab

Say "stripe."
    Say "stripe" without the / s /.   tripe

Say "flush."
    Change the vowel sound to / $\breve{a}$ /.   flash

***Figure 9.* Sample phoneme deletion and substitution drills.**

English Word Construction

For students with reading difficulties, understanding how words in the English code are constructed can be advantageous to improving their reading skills. The English language, like many of the approximately 2,700 spoken and written languages in the world, is composed of a mixture of other linguistic influences. Specifically, the linguistic influences upon English come in the form of how we construct the words that compose our spoken and written language. The three main linguistic models of word construction that constitute the English language are:

- Latinate word construction (55%),

- Anglo-Saxon word construction (25%), and

- Greek word construction (11%).

Figure 10 shows the composition of the English language presented in pie chart form. You can see that Latinate word construction constitutes 55% of the pie. In other words, a little more than one out of every two words in our language is based upon Latinate word construction.

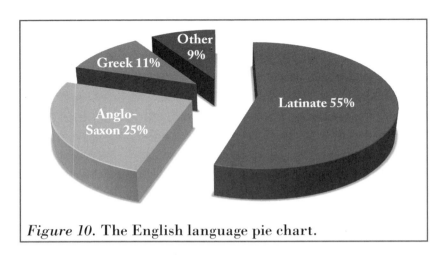

Figure 10. The English language pie chart.

Anglo-Saxon word construction constitutes 25% of our language. One out of every four words in our language is based upon Anglo-Saxon word construction; however, please note that Anglo-Saxon word construction occupies nearly 100% of all words learned through the third grade. As a result, knowledge of Anglo-Saxon word construction forms a critical foundation for reading and spelling the English language.

Greek word construction constitutes 11% of our language. A little more than one out of every 10 words in our language is based upon Greek word construction. It bears mentioning, though, that most of the advanced vocabulary from mathematics and the sciences are based upon Greek word construction. Additionally, there are vocabulary words from math and the sciences that are hybrids between Greek word construction and Latinate word construction.

Teaching students to understand how words are constructed includes the study of roots, prefixes, suffixes, and spelling rules to increase students' reading and spelling skills. Many commercial products are available to teach students to understand vocabulary by breaking it into its parts. However, for teachers and parents interested in creating their own materials to help students learn word construction, Chapter 5 is invaluable for understanding the various types of word construction and many of the spelling rules inherent in our language.

In addition, the chapter points to several of the appendices of this book for further tools to use in teaching the various roots, suffixes, and prefixes. Teachers can implement these kinds of studies with gifted students, as well, who often enjoy learning how words are constructed. One way to engage all learners in a classroom in such study is to present a word of the day, broken into its various parts. In addition, teachers can motivate students to learn roots by suggesting that they learn either a few roots or a larger vocabulary list. In my experience, students will always choose to learn the roots!

Orton-Gillingham Approach

The Orton-Gillingham approach is a unique language training system that was designed by Dr. Samuel Orton and Anna Gillingham. Dr. Orton, a neuropsychiatrist and pathologist, was a pioneer in focusing attention on reading failure and related language processing difficulties. He revolutionized modern thought concerning learning disabilities, determining that language-based disorders were biological and not environmental in origin. He extensively studied children with language processing difficulties and formulated a set of teaching principles and practices for such children.

Anna Gillingham was a gifted educator, psychologist, and school administrator. Working with Dr. Orton, she devised methods of teaching these students based on the principles formulated by Dr. Orton, and she published *The Gillingham Manual*, which she wrote with Bessie Stillman.

The Orton-Gillingham approach revolves around the scientifically based concepts that humans acquire and master language through three distinct neurological pathways: visual processing (seeing), auditory processing (hearing), and tactile-kinesthetic processing (feeling). In the last pathway, tactile refers to small muscle movements (e.g., handwriting, manipulation of the vocal tract, tying a shoelace), and kinesthetic refers to large muscle movements (e.g., movement of the arms or legs). The Orton-Gillingham approach incorporates all three pathways (visual, auditory, and tactile-kinesthetic) in the remediation of language skills or in primary language instruction.

We have previously discussed the visual and auditory neurological pathways and their impact on language acquisition and processing. What remains to be explored is tactile-kinesthetic processing. Tactile-kinesthetic ability refers to motor movements, and there are two classes: *tactile*, or fine motor (e.g., speech production, handwriting, typing), and *kinesthetic*, or gross motor (e.g., running, athletics). Motor memory is a very powerful tool. Physical activities, such as riding a bicycle, remain in active memory once the skill has been acquired, despite the time lapse that occurs between rides. Therefore, the movements of the hand while writing and the movements of the speech organs and vocal tract during phoneme or word production provide a crucial pathway of the learning process. The area of the language brain that controls the vocal tract is called Broca's area (see Figure 11). Broca's area is located on the inferior frontal gyrus in the frontal lobe. It is the speech center of the language brain, as it directs the muscles of the jaw, tongue, and throat to form the sounds that make up words.

The Orton-Gillingham approach incorporates all three pathways from start to finish. During one component of an Orton-Gillingham session, a student will look at a letter or phonogram and make the corresponding sound. In a reverse process, the student will hear a sound and must name and form the associated letter or phonogram. Sound-symbol correspondence must be systematically and explicitly taught. It must be firmly established in a logical progression from single vowels and consonants through consonant and vowel pairs (digraphs and diphthongs). The sequence is always from the simple to complex. Even within this vital, yet short, portion of the Orton-Gillingham session, all three neurological pathways are incorporated into the learning process.

The Orton-Gillingham approach is an intensive, sequential phonics-based system that teaches the basics of word formation before whole meanings. The approach accommodates and utilizes the three learning pathways through which people learn, and it teaches to a stu-

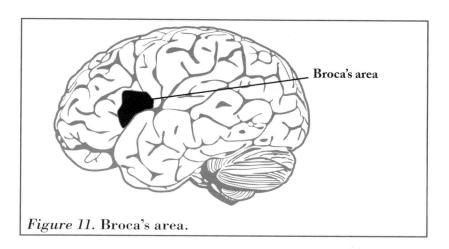

Figure 11. Broca's area.

dent's strengths while seeking to improve weaknesses through explicit and systematic phonics instruction. The approach will foster in your child the ability to forensically master reading, writing, and spelling. The approach is ideal for traditional school settings or for parents who want to personally tutor their children in homeschool environments. The Orton-Gillingham approach has been the most powerful intervention designed expressly for the remediation of the language processing problems of children and adults who struggle with reading, writing, and spelling due to auditory and visual processing deficits caused by a language-based learning disorder. However, due to the approach's design and manner of implementation, research supports that all students can and will benefit from its multisensory approach. The Orton-Gillingham process places students in position to master the 85% of the English code that is phonetic. Further, and most importantly, it allows them to make intelligent choices toward mastering the remaining 15% of the English code that must be analyzed in order to be applied properly.

A detailed, structured plan for using the Orton-Gillingham approach is available in Chapter 6 for parents and teachers interested in trying this approach for one-on-one remediation. The Orton-Gillingham approach as presented in that chapter is:

- **Language-based:** The Orton-Gillingham approach is based on a technique of studying and teaching language, understanding the nature of human language, the mechanisms involved in learning, and the language-learning processes in individuals.

- **Multisensory:** Orton-Gillingham teaching sessions are action-oriented with auditory, visual, and tactile-kinesthetic elements reinforcing each other for optimal learning. The student learns spelling simultaneously with reading.

- **Structured, Sequential, and Cumulative:** The Orton-Gillingham teacher introduces the elements of the language systematically. Students begin by reading and writing sounds in isolation. Then, they blend the sounds into syllables and words. Students learn the elements of language (e.g., consonants, vowels, digraphs, blends, diphthongs) in an orderly fashion. The student then proceeds to advanced structural elements such as syllable types, roots, and affixes. As students learn new material, they continue to review old material to the level of automaticity. The teacher addresses vocabulary, sentence structure, composition, and reading comprehension in a similar structured, sequential, and cumulative manner.

- **Cognitive:** Students learn about the history of the English language and study the many generalizations and rules that govern its structure. Students also become aware of the neurological pathway that serves their learning style best. This fosters the ability to learn and apply the language knowledge necessary for achieving reading and writing competencies.

- **Emotionally Sound:** In every lesson, the student experiences a high degree of success and gains confidence as well as skills. Learning becomes a rewarding and happy experience.

- **Diagnostic-Prescriptive:** The method is infinitely adaptable. Students are taught only what they require, in the manner that is appropriate for that particular student.

Again, for parents and teachers interested in utilizing this approach, I suggest that you read Chapter 6 and try out the structured plan I've created for reading remediation based on the Orton-Gillingham approach.

Chapter Summary

These general strategies will provide some relief to students who are struggling with the reading process. The next chapter moves forward and provides parents and teachers with a solid foundation of the English code by examining how vowels, consonants, and sounds create words.

chapter 4

How Sounds Are Constructed: Understanding Consonants and Vowels

I have included the following information for the edification of parents and teachers. The information that I have gained over 27 years in education has served to strengthen my grasp of the articulation process and its inseparable relationship to phonemic awareness. Please keep in mind that our intention is to provide language remediation using a multisensory approach. We wish to engage all three neurological pathways in the process. Further, the third neurological pathway, tactile-kinesthetic processing, involves small muscle movements such as those found in the tract of articulation (tactile) as well as large muscle movements (kinesthetic). Parents and teachers themselves must become familiar with the process of articulation and its inseparable relationship to phonemic awareness in order to foster the development of this skill in students.

The 44 Phonemes in the English Language

Each language has its prerequisite number of sounds (phonemes). In the English language, there are 44: five short vowel sounds, five long vowel sounds, six r-controlled vowel sounds, four advanced vowel sounds, 18 basic consonant sounds, and six advanced consonant sounds. See Table 2 for a breakdown of these phonemes.

Most letters of the alphabet are symbols for a single phoneme (speech sound). However, there are exceptions. The letter "c" can make the / k / sound, as in "king," or the / s /, as in "silly." The letter "g" can make the / g / sound, as in "go," or the / j /, as in "jelly." The letter "s" can make the / s /, as in "silly," or the / z / in "nose." The letter "x" represents two phonemes, the / k / and / s / sounds. The sounds are pronounced in sequence. The / k / sound is immediately followed by the / s / sound, as in the word "box." When the letter "x" begins a word, it makes the / z / sound, as in "xylophone." Also, "qu" represents two sounds, the / k / sound immediately followed by the / w / sound. It is important to note that the letter "q" is never found in the English language without being immediately followed by the letter "u" (e.g., "queen," "quiet," "quick," "quack").

Classification of Sounds

There are two main categories of articulated sounds, *nasal* and *oral*. Nasal sounds (/ m /, / n /, and / ng /) are sounds produced when the soft palate or velum (see Figure 12) is not in its raised position, allowing air to escape through both the nose and the mouth. Oral sounds are sounds produced with the velum up, blocking the air from escaping through the nose.

Table 2

English Language Phonemes (Sounds)

Sound Type	Sounds	
short vowel sounds	/ ă / as in "hat" / ĕ / as in "bed" / ĭ / as in "fish"	/ ŏ / as in "stop" / ŭ / as in "cup"
long vowel sounds	/ ā / as in "skate" / ē / as in "Pete" / ī / as in "kite"	/ ō / as in "note" / ū / as in "flute"
r-controlled vowel sounds	/ er / as in "herd" / ar / as in "car" / or / as in "born"	/ ear / as in "fear" / air / as in "hair" / oor / as in "floor"
advanced vowel sounds	/ oo / as in "book" / ow / as in "cow"	/ oy / as in "boy" / aw / as in "saw"
basic consonant sounds	/ b / as in "big" / d / as in "dog" / f / as in "fish" / g / as in "go" / h / as in "hat" / j / as in "jelly" / k / as in "king" / l / as in "lips" / m / as in "man"	/ n / as in "no" / p / as in "pan" / r / as in "rabbit" / s / as in "silly" / t / as in "test" / v / as in "van" / w / as in "win" / y / as in "yellow" / z / as in "zipper"
advanced consonant sounds	/ sh / as in "shut" / ch / as in "chin" / zh / as in "measure"	/ ng / as in "thing" / th / as in "thimble" / th / as in "this"

The Tools of Articulation

Consonants are categorized by three criteria:

- voiced or unvoiced,

- place of articulation, and

- manner of articulation.

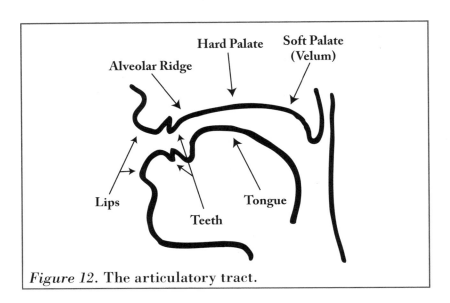

Figure 12. The articulatory tract.

A *voiced sound* is produced when the vocal cords are together during airflow. The air forces its way through, causing the vocal cords to vibrate. A voiced sound may be vocalized as loudly as the speaker wishes, even screamed. Conversely, an *unvoiced sound* is produced when the vocal cords are apart during airflow. This allows the air to flow freely through the glottis and supraglottal cavities. An unvoiced sound may not be screamed, regardless of the effort of the speaker.

Place of articulation is the localization of the speech mechanism to a specific feature of the articulatory tract (see Figure 12 for a diagram of the articulatory tract). There are 10 places of articulation:

1. the two lips pressed together (bilabial),

2. the tongue tip placed firmly against the alveolar ridge (lingua-alveolar),

3. the tongue backed up into the soft palate (velum and lingua-velar),

4. the upper row of teeth placed across the tip of the bottom lip (labio-dental),

5. the tongue placed between the rows of teeth (lingua-interdental),

6. the tongue tip placed against the gum ridge (lingua-alveolar),

7. the tongue blade placed against the back of the gum ridge (lingua-palatal),

8. the glottis (glottal),

9. the tongue tip and blade placed against the back of the gum ridge (lingua-palatal), and

10. neutral position.

As evidenced by the places of articulation, the tongue is the most important articulator. It is an extremely powerful muscle, and it is the only muscle that is attached in only one location. The second most important articulator is the alveolar ridge.

Manner of articulation is determined by airflow through the oral or nasal cavities and place of articulation. The two major divisions are stops and continuants. Stops are consonant sounds in which there is an airstream stoppage in the oral cavity. Continuants are consonant sounds where there is no airstream stoppage in the oral cavity.

Stops and continuants are further subdivided as follows:

- **plosives:** oral stops in which air pressure is rapidly released when the mouth is opened, such as:
  - bilabial stops: / p / / b /
  - lingua-alveolar stops: / t / / d /
  - lingua-velar stops: / k / / g /

- **fricatives:** continuants in which the airflow is so severely obstructed that it cases friction, such as
  - labio-dental fricatives: / f / / v /
  - lingua-alveolar fricatives: / s / / z /
  - lingua-interdental fricatives: / th / / _th_ /

- lingua-palatal fricatives: / *sh* / / *zh* /

- **affricates:** produced by a stop closure followed by an imme-diate, gradual release of the closure of the oral cavity. It is a combination of a stop and a fricative. For example, / *ch* / is a combination of / *t* / and / *sh* / and / *j* / is a combination of / *d* / and / *zh* /.

- **liquids:** voiced sounds produced by partial obstruction of the airstream in the mouth. There is not, however, enough obstruction to cause any real constriction or friction. These include:

  - lingua-alveolar liquid: / *l* /

  - neutral position: / *r* /

- **glides:** sounds produced by moving the tongue rapidly in a gliding fashion either toward or away from a neighboring vowel. They are always preceded or followed by a vowel and include:

  - lingua-palatal glide: / *y* /

  - bilabial glide: / *w* /

- **nasals:** sounds produced as air is emitted through the nasal cavity, such as:

  - bilabial nasal: / *m* /

  - lingua-alveolar nasal: / *n* /

  - lingua-velar nasal: / *ng* /

Understanding Consonants

The 21 consonants in the English language take on various sounds and pronunciations. Table 3 provides a breakdown of each consonant, its pronunciation, and a key word for each consonant. The table also shares some notes for when the pronunciations of consonants differ.

The specific articulation of consonants takes place using different parts of the articulatory tract. Knowledge of the oral mechanics required to generate consonant sounds provides students with an additional tactile tool as manipulation of the tract of articulation allows students struggling with auditory discrimination issues to better isolate individual sounds. For example, if students feel the back of the tongue rise to the velum (hard palate) and move forward, scraping gently, there are only two sounds that may be generated using this sequence of oral movements: the "k" or the "g."

The consonants are articulated in the following manner:

- */ p /, / b /,* **and** */ m /*: The bilabials (/ *p* /, / *b* /, and / *m* /) are articulated by pressing both lips together. For the unvoiced / *p* /, the lips are closed. Slight air pressure is built up. A light puff of air is exploded through the oral cavity by the sudden parting of the lips. Voice is added for / *b* /. For / *m* /, the voiced breath stream is emitted through the nasal cavity.

- */ f /* **and** */ v /*: The labio-dentals (/ *f* / and / *v* /) are articulated by touching the bottom lip to the upper teeth. For / *f* /, the lower lip approximates the upper incisors. Friction is created as air is emitted through the oral cavity between the teeth and lip. For / *v* /, a greater amount of tension between the lip and teeth is created.

- */ th /* **and** */ t̲h̲ /*: The lingua-interdentals (/ *th* / and / *t̲h̲* /) are articulated by inserting the tip of the tongue between the upper and lower teeth. For / *th* /, the tongue blade, in a relaxed and broad manner, protrudes slightly between the two rows of teeth. The air stream passes through the oral cavity between the tongue and the teeth. For / *t̲h̲* /, voice is added as the air stream passes between the tongue and teeth.

Table 3

Consonants at a Glance

Consonant	Key Word	Pronunciation Symbol
b	as in "bat"	/ b /
c	as in "cat"	/ k /*
d	as in "dog"	/ d /
f	as in "fish"	/ f /
g	as in "game"	/ g /**
h	as in "hat"	/ h /
j	as in "jam"	/ j /
k	as in "kite"	/ k /
l	as in "lamp"	/ l /
m	as in "man"	/ m /
n	as in "nest"	/ n /
p	as in "pig"	/ p /
qu	as in "queen"	/ kw /***
r	as in "rat"	/ r /
s	as in "sock"	/ s /****
t	as in "top"	/ t /
v	as in "van"	/ v /
w	as in "wagon"	/ w /
x	as in "box"	/ ks /*****
y	as in "yellow"	/ y /
z	as in "zipper"	/ z /

Notes:
* "c" says / s / when placed before "e, " "i, " or "y" (e.g., "cement," "cider," "cycle")
** "g" says / j / when placed before "e, " "i, " or "y" (e.g., "gymnastics," "gem," "gin")
*** In English, "q" never appears without "u" immediately following it (e.g., "quack," "quail")
**** "s" says / z / when found between two vowels (e.g., "reason," "season," "treason")
***** "x" says / gz / when placed before a vowel other than "y" (e.g., "exam," "example," "exit")

- **/ t /, / d /, / n /, / s /, / z /, and / l /**: The lingua-alveolars (/ t /, / d /, / n /, / s /, / z /, and / l /) are articulated by raising the front part of the tongue to the alveolar ridge. For the / t / sound, the tip of the tongue is placed firmly against the alveolar ridge. Air pressure is built up, and a light puff of air is exploded by the sudden drop of the tongue. For / d /, voice is added to the / t /. For / s /, the tongue is placed against the alveolar ridge. Air flows through a small aperture and out of the oral cavity, producing a hissing sound. For / z /, voice is added to the / s /. For / n /, the tongue is in the position as for / t / with the tip of the tongue against the alveolar ridge. A voiced airstream is emitted through the nasal cavity. Finally, for / l /, the tongue blade is broad. It is fitted lightly against the alveolar ridge. Voice is emitted through the oral cavity around the tongue and out of the mouth.

- / sh /, / ch /, / zh /, and / j /: The lingua-palatals (/ sh /, / ch /, / zh /, and / j /) are articulated by raising the front part of the tongue to a point on the hard palate just behind the alveolar ridge. For / sh /, the lips are slightly rounded and protruded. The tongue is broadened to touch the molars on each side. The tongue blade approximates sides of the alveolar ridge. An aperture larger than that for / s / is formed down the middle of the tongue. Air is forced through the oral cavity, down the aperture. Sound is produced as the air passes through the aperture. For / zh /, voice is added to / sh /. For / ch /, the lips are slightly rounded and the tongue is broadened along the alveolar ridge and touching molars on each side as for / sh /. Air pressure is built up and exploded by suddenly dropping the tongue and the jaw. For / j /, voice is added to / ch /.

- / k /, / g /, and / ng /: Lingua-velars (/ k /, / g /, and / ng /) are articulated by raising the back of the tongue to the soft palate or velum. For / k /, the tongue tip is at the base of the lower teeth. The back of the tongue rises to contact the soft palate (velum). Air pressure is released by the sudden dropping of the tongue. For / g /, voice is added as air pressure is added. For / ng /, a voiced air stream is emitted through the nasal cavity.

- / h /: The glottal (/ h /) is articulated through the open glottis. A light flow of air is emitted from the mouth. The position of the lips and tongue and the degree of mouth opening will be influenced by the vowel that follows / *h* /.

- **/ *wh* / and / *w* /:** The bilabial positions, / *wh* / and / *w* /, are not true sounds. They are formations of the mouth accompanied by airflow as the mouth prepares to form the sound of the vowel that is to follow. For / *wh* /, the lips are slightly rounded and protruded. The tongue tip is down. Air flows through the oral cavity, over the contour of the tongue and out of the mouth. For / *w* /, the lips are slightly protruded and rounded as for / *wh* /, although / *w* / requires less air flow. Voice is emitted for both positions through the oral cavity just before the lips move to the position of the vowel sound that follows.

- **/ *y* /:** The lingua-palatal glide, / *y* /, produces a sound identical to the long vowel / *ē* / that is found in the word "tree." It is articulated with the tongue tip down. The sides of the tongue blade touch the molars on each side. A small aperture is formed down the middle of the tongue. Voice passes through this aperture and friction is produced. The long vowel / *ē* / glides into the next sound that follows the letter "y."

Consonants can be combined in the English language in multiple ways: digraphs, blends, and clusters. You have probably noticed that many of the drills for teaching children phonemic awareness and mediating their reading skills ask students to identify these different types of consonant combinations.

Consonant Digraphs

A consonant digraph is two consonants that work together to produce one sound. We abandon the sounds of the individual consonants for the generation of a new sound. Therefore, the consonant digraph is considered a single phoneme.[3] A consonant digraph may appear in the beginning, middle, or end of a word.

---

3   For clarity, I do not view "-ck" and "-ck-" as digraphs. As dictated by the Long Spelling Rule, they represent the long spelling for / *k* / when the / *k* / sound immediately follows a short vowel.

The six consonant digraphs are "ch," "ph," "sh," "th" (soft or unvoiced), "th" (hard or voiced), and "wh." Notice the application of these digraphs in words like "chief," "telephone," "sham," "thief," "father," and "whip." A full list of various words that can be used to teach the consonant digraphs to students has been included on a special website for this book: http://www.prufrock.com/assets/clientpages/schoolsuccessdyslexia.aspx. At this site, you can download a complete list to help you make the drill cards you'll need to teach students each of the individual concepts discussed in this chapter (see Chapter 6 for more information on creating drill cards for use with the structured approach to reading remediation that I recommend).

Consonant Blends

A consonant blend is composed of two consonants that work together as a pair (when three consonants work together, it's considered a consonant cluster). Each consonant maintains its individual sound. The consonant blend may appear at the beginning or the end of a word. If it appears in the beginning of a word, it is an initial blend. If it appears at the end of a word, it is a final blend.

Initial Blends

In the English code, most initial blends that are pairs are created using the letters "l," "r," or "s." Notice the applications and locations of the initial blends created with the letter "l" in the following words: "blue," "clap," "fly," "glass," "plow," and "sleep." Notice the applications and locations of the initial blends created with the letter "r" in the following words: "brick," "crown," "frown," "grass," "prod," and "tree." Notice the applications and locations of the initial blends created with the letter "s" in the following words: "scoot," "skin," "stew," "smock," "snow," "slip," "swell," "spin," and "squad."

In the English code, there are two blends that resemble initial consonant clusters that work together as a pair, "shr-" and "thr-". Each is composed of a consonant digraph followed by an additional consonant. Remember that a consonant digraph consists of two consonants that work together to produce one new sound. Together, the digraph and additional consonant function as a pair to form an initial blend. Notice the applications and locations of the initial blends "shr-" and "thr-" in the following words: "shrink," "thread," "shroud," "throw," "shrew," and "throng."

A full list of various words that can be used to teach the initial blends to students can be found at http://www.prufrock.com/assets/clientpages/schoolsuccessdyslexia.aspx.

Final Blends

Most final blends in the English code that are pairs are created using the letters "l," "n," "s," or "t." Notice the applications and locations of the final blends created with the letter "l" in the following words: "belt," "milk," "welp," "salt," "old," and "shelf." Notice the applications and locations of the final blends created with the letter "n" in the following words: "band," "think," "went," "hunt," "sunk," and "grand." Notice the applications and locations of the final blends created with the letter "s" in the following words: "dusk," "wasp," "west," "whisper," "blister," and "frisk." Notice the applications and locations of the final blends created with the letter "t" in the following words: "fact," "swift," "went," "wept," and "west."

There is one final blend that is created with the letter "m": "-mp." From this final blend, we get words like "jump," "frump," and "dump."

In the English code, there is one final blend that works together as a pair, yet resembles a consonant cluster: "-nch." It is composed of a consonant digraph followed by an additional consonant. Remember that a consonant digraph consists of two consonants that work together to produce one sound. Together, the digraph and additional consonant function as a pair to form an initial blend. From this final blend, we get words like "ranch," "wench," and "clinch."

A full list of various words that can be used to teach the final blends to students can be found at http://www.prufrock.com/assets/clientpages/schoolsuccessdyslexia.aspx.

Consonant Clusters

Consonant clusters may appear as initial triple blends or final triple blends. Initial triple blends in the English code are created using the letter "s." Notice the applications and locations of the initial triple blends created with the letter "s" in the following words: "scream," "split," "sprint," "string," and "splash."

There are two final consonant clusters, "-mpt" and "-nct." From the final cluster "-mpt," we get words like "tempt," "prompt," and "exempt." From the final cluster "-nct," we get words like "instinct," "precinct," and "succinct."

A full list of various words that can be used to teach the consonant clusters to students can be found at http://www.prufrock.com/assets/clientpages/schoolsuccessdyslexia.aspx.

Short Vowels

The articulation of vowels differs from that of consonants in that:

- all vowels are continuants,

- all vowels are voiced, and

- all vowels are produced through the oral cavity.

Vowels are produced by an unobstructed flow of air, and they function as the pulse or beat of a syllable. The rhythmic function of vowels is so instrumental that every syllable in the English language has at least one vowel sound.

As in the construction of consonant phonemes, the tongue, again, is the most important articulator in the production of vowel phonemes. However, the alveolar ridge does not play a role in vowel phoneme production. Instead, the second most important articulator in vowel phoneme production is the shape of the oral cavity, the mouth.

Short vowel phonemes differ greatly from long vowel phonemes.[4] Where long vowel phonemes say the names of the letter, short vowel phonemes do not. The five short vowel phonemes are:

- /ă/ as in "hat" (/h//ă//t/): To generate the short "a" sound, there is a slight arching of the tongue blade in the middle. The edges of the tongue blade may come in contact with the upper molars. The tip of the tongue is at the base of the lower front teeth. The jaw is lower as the mouth is opened more than for /ĭ/ as voice is emitted. Notice the applications and locations of the short "a" sound in the following words: "lap," "flat," "dab," "ham," "mad," "tan," and "lash."

- /ĕ/ as in "bed" (/b//ĕ//d/): To generate the short "e" sound, the tongue contour is slightly lower, the lips are more relaxed, and the jaw opening is slightly larger than for the /ĭ/ as voice is emitted. Notice the applications and locations of the short "e" sound in the following words: "fed," "lent," "hemp," "den," "vest," "pet," "left," and "kelp."

- /ĭ/ as in "fish" (/f//ĭ//sh/): To generate the short "i" sound, the front of the tongue blade is high. The jaw begins to open slightly. The tongue forms an aperture slightly larger than that for /ē/ because it is lowered and the jaw is opened slightly. The tongue tip is at or near the base of the lower front teeth as voice is emitted. Notice the applications and locations of the short "i " sound in the following words: "wish," "hint," "crimp," "list," "pick," "lift," "pit," "fix," and "skid."

- /ŏ/ as in "stop" (/s//t//ŏ//p/): In the generation of the short "o" sound, there is almost no elevation of the tongue during the generation of this sound. The mouth is open slightly.

4   Short vowels are always found in *closed* syllables. See the Syllable Types section on page 84.

The lips are not as rounded as for the / *aw* /, voice is emitted, and the sound is shorter than / *aw* /. Notice the applications and locations of the short "o" sound in the following words: "lot," "pond," "mob," "trot," "fox," "loft," and "drop."

- /*ŭ*/ **as in "cup"** (/ *c* / / *ŭ* / / *p* /): To generate the short "u" sound, there is a slight arching of the tongue blade in the middle. The edges of the tongue blade may come in contact with the upper molars. The tip of the tongue is at the base of the lower front teeth as voice is emitted. Notice the applications and locations of the short "u" sound in the following words: "hug," "hunt," "jump," "rust," "gun," "rum," "mush," "cult," and "puck."

A full list of various words that can be used to teach the short vowels to students can be found at http://www.prufrock.com/assets/clientpages/schoolsuccessdyslexia.aspx.

Long Vowels and Long Vowel Spellings

Long vowel phonemes differ greatly from short vowel phonemes. Long vowel phonemes say the names of the letter, where short vowel phonemes do not. The five long vowel sounds are:

- /*ā*/ **as in "mate"** (/ *m* / / *ā* / / *t* /): To generate the long "a" phoneme, please note that, like the / *ī* /, the long / *ā* / is a vowel glide or diphthong. To generate the / *ā* / diphthong, the elevation of the tongue is low, nearing the floor of the mouth. The lips are slightly rounded. The mouth is slightly more open than for the / *ĕ* /. The chin is at the same position as for the / *ī* /, and voice is emitted. After the generation of the initial phoneme, the lips contract and the jaw and tongue rise as the / *ē* / phoneme is produced.

- /*ē*/ **as in "beef"** (/ *b* / / *ē* / / *f* /): To generate the long "e" sound, the tongue is placed in the most forward and highest point possible. The tongue is at the base of the lower front teeth. The front part of the tongue blade is high. The sides of the tongue are against the molars. The corners of the mouth are drawn back, as if in a smile, and there is a slight space between the upper and lower teeth as voice is emitted.

- */ī/* **as in "kite"** (*/k//ī//t/*): Note that the long vowel / ī / is a diphthong or a vowel glide. To generate the / ī / diphthong, the elevation of the tongue is low, nearing the floor of the mouth. The mouth is slightly more open than for the / ŏ /. The chin is at the second lowest position as voice is emitted. After the generation of the initial phoneme, the lips contract, and the jaw and tongue rise as the vowel, / ē /, is produced.

- */ō/* **as in "note"** (*/n//ō//t/*): The phoneme / ō / is a diphthong or a vowel glide. A vowel glide begins as one sound and ends with another. To generate the / ō / diphthong, the elevation of the tongue is low, nearing the floor of the mouth. The lips are rounded. The mouth is slightly less open than for the short / ŏ /. The chin is at the second lowest position as voice is emitted. After the generation of the initial phoneme, the lips contract as if to make the / w /. The change in mouth position generates the proper end to the / ō / phoneme.

- */ū/* **as in "mule"** (*/m//ū//l/*) **or** */oo/* **as in "too"** (*/t//oo/*): The / ē / / oo / sound is a hybrid of the / ē / and the / oo /. The tongue is elevated at beginning of the sound. The mouth is open slightly. The lips are not rounded. After the / ē / has been generated, the lips round slightly and the jaw rises. A very small aperture is formed down the middle of the tongue, and / oo / is emitted through this aperture. For the / oo / sound, the lips are slightly rounded, and the tongue tip is at the base of the lower teeth. The back of the tongue is high. A very small aperture is formed down the middle of the tongue. Voice is emitted through this aperture.

Long Vowel Spellings

Long vowel spellings are designated by the location of the phoneme within the word. There are four classes of long vowel spellings:

- open syllables;

- one-syllable word construction, also known as vowel + consonant + "e" or v-e (e.g., "a-e," "e-e");

- middle of the word spellings, also known as middle spellings; and

- end of the word spellings, also known as end spellings.

Because long vowel spellings are used based upon where the long vowel sound is found in a word, we now can create a matrix. Figure 13 shows what our beginning matrix will look like. Now let's examine each of the four long vowel spellings.

Open syllable spellings. Open syllables are syllables that end with a long vowel. For example, please note that the following sequence ends with a vowel.

ma

When "a" is located at the end of an open syllable, it is naturally long. It must say / $\bar{a}$ / as in "major." To clarify, all that is required to make the vowel long is to have it be located at the end of the syllable. The following open syllables all contain long vowels:

- "ma" as in "major"

- "me" as in "meter"

- "mi" as in "minor"

- "mo" as in "motor"

- "mu" as in "music"

Vowels	Open Spellings	V-E Spellings	Middle Spellings	End Spellings
a				
e				
i				
o				
u				

Figure 13. Beginning long vowel spelling matrix.

It is important to note that in the English code, open syllables are generally a part of multisyllabic words (words with two syllables or more). Words like "he," "she," "we," "go," "so," or "no" are exceptions to the rule. Nevertheless, based upon our explanation of open syllables, we may add spellings to our long vowel spelling matrix. Our matrix now looks like Figure 14.

One-syllable word spellings. One-syllable word spellings are composed of a vowel + a consonant + a silent "e" (or "v-e"). For example, please note the v-e construction in the following word:

mate

We can clearly see that the word ends with a silent "e" that is separated from the vowel by a consonant. The purpose of the silent "e" is to make the vowel long. Here, the "a" must say / $\bar{a}$ /. Therefore, the above sequence must say /m / / $\bar{a}$ / / t /. To clarify, all that is required to make a single vowel long in a one-syllable word is to have a silent "e" located at the end of the syllable. The following v-e syllables all contain long vowels:

- mate

- mete

- mite

- mote

- mute

Vowels	Open Spellings	V-E Spellings	Middle Spellings	End Spellings
a	a			
e	e			
i	i			
o	o			
u	u			

Figure 14. Updated long vowel spelling matrix.

It is important to note that in the English code, v-e construction should be the student's first choice when spelling one-syllable words. Further, based upon our explanation of open syllables, we may add spellings to our long vowel spelling matrix. Our matrix now looks like Figure 15.

Middle of the word spellings. These spellings are those used when the long vowel sound is located in the middle of a one-syllable word. Unfortunately, where open syllable spellings and one-syllable word spellings each follow a pattern, middle of the word spellings do not. For each long vowel sound in middle spellings, the spelling is different.

- For long vowel "a," we use "ai," as in "pain."

- For long vowel "e," we use "ee" and "ea,"[5] as in "meet" and "meat."

- For long vowel "i," we use "igh," as in "night."

- For long vowel "o," we use "oa," as in "boat."

- For long vowel "u," there is no middle spelling.

Again, in the English code, "middle of the word" spellings are used when the long vowel sound is in the middle of a one syllable word. Now, let's update our matrix to match Figure 16.

---

5   The middle spelling for the long "e" phoneme also functions as an end spelling in some words.

Vowels	Open Spellings	V-E Spellings	Middle Spellings	End Spellings
a	a	a-e		
e	e	e-e		
i	i	i-e		
o	o	o-e		
u	u	u-e		

Figure 15. Updated long vowel spelling matrix.

Vowels	Open Spellings	V-E Spellings	Middle Spellings	End Spellings
a	a	a-e	ai	
e	e	e-e	ee, ea	
i	i	i-e	igh	
o	o	o-e	oa	
u	u	u-e		

Figure 16. Updated long vowel spelling matrix.

End of the word spellings. End spellings are those used when the long vowel sound is located at the end of a one-syllable word. Unfortunately, where open syllable spellings and one-syllable word spellings each follow a pattern, end spellings do not. For each long vowel sound in end spellings, the spelling is different.

- For long vowel "a," we use "ay," as in "pay."

- For long vowel "e," we use "ee" and "ea," as in "see" or "sea."

- For long vowel "i," we use "y," as in "sky."

- For long vowel "o," we use "ow," as in "slow."

- For long vowel "u," we use "ue" and "ew," as in "due" and "dew."

Vowels	Open Spellings	V-E Spellings	Middle Spellings	End Spellings
a	a	a-e	ai	ay
e	e	e-e	ee, ea	ee, ea
i	i	i-e	igh	y
o	o	o-e	oa	ow
u	u	u-e		ue, ew

Figure 17. Completed long vowel spelling matrix.

Again, in the English code, end spellings are used when the long vowel sound is at the end of a one-syllable word. Now, let's update our matrix one last time as in Figure 17.

As we examine our matrix, we see obvious patterns in the open syllables spellings and the v-e spellings. What may prove problematic for teachers, parents, and students is remembering the middle and end spellings. Not to worry. There's an excellent mnemonic to assist you. It goes like this:

There once was a group of little boys who had a sailboat and a dream. One night, they decided to s**ai**l a**way** to s**ee** the s**ea**. While sailing, they looked up and saw a beautiful n**igh**t sk**y**. Well, they knew that had to get home before their parents awoke. But they had a problem. Their b**oa**t was too sl**ow**. So, the boys called the Coast Guard who came to resc**ue** the cr**ew**.

Fairly straightforward, wouldn't you agree? Let's take a look at the key elements of our story.

- s**ai**l a**way** = "ai" and "ay"
- s**ee** the s**ea** = "ee" and "ea"
- n**igh**t sk**y** = "igh" and "y"
- b**oa**t was sl**ow** = "oa" and "ow"
- resc**ue** the cr**ew** = "ue" and "ew"

Mastering the 20 different long vowel spellings will prove invaluable to readers and spellers, as they will aid in visual recognition as well as recall when encoding. Until students master the spellings, students should be asked to create the long vowel spelling matrix as part of their nightly homework assignments. Additionally, students should be asked to create the long vowel spelling matrix and cursive alphabet each day as class or tutoring time begins. (See the arguments that support having students write in cursive on p. 163.)

Long Vowel Spelling Drills

Putting the knowledge of long vowel spellings into action is simple using a rudimentary drill. Merely create a blank matrix, and fill it in using a process of deductive reasoning. Let me explain. As we have studied, the correct long vowel spelling is determined by the location of the long vowel sound in the word. All we have to do is listen to where the long vowel sound is found, and using deductive reasoning, we can easily find which spelling is correct.

Let's start with the long vowel spellings for "a." Specifically, let's start with the word "play." In order to work through the process, we listen carefully to the pronunciation of the word. Then, we ask ourselves, can the word "play" be placed in category 1, the open syllable spelling category? Well, remember that the open syllable category is reserved for words with two or more syllables. The word "play" has only one syllable, so we know that the word "play" cannot go into the open syllable category; it cannot be spelled, "p-l-a." So, we place an "X" in the square reserved for open syllable spellings. Next, we ask ourselves if the word can fit in category 2, the v-e category. We remember that the v-e category requires that a consonant separate the vowel from the silent "e." In other words, there needs to be a consonant sound after the long vowel sound. Clearly, when we pronounce "play," we hear that there is no consonant after the vowel. Therefore, we know that it cannot be placed in category 2, and it cannot be spelled "p-l-a-e." So, we place an "X" in the square reserved for v-e spellings. Next, we ask ourselves if the word can fit in category 3, the middle spell-

Vowels	Open Spellings	V-E Spellings	Middle Spellings	End Spellings
a	X	X	X	ay
e				
i				
o				
u				

Figure 18. Completed matrix for the word "play."

ing category. We remember that the middle spelling category requires that the vowel sound be located in the middle of the word. As we determined, the long vowel "a" sound is not located in the middle of the word. Therefore, we know that it cannot be placed in category 3, and it cannot be spelled, "p-l-a-i ." So, we place an "X" in the square reserved for middle spellings. Finally, when pronouncing the word, we clearly hear that the long vowel "a" sound is located at the end of the word. As a result, there is only one correct way to spell the word, "p-l-**ay**." Therefore, our completed long vowel spelling matrix for long vowel "a" (the word "play") will look like Figure 18.

Following the same process, we find that there is only one way to spell the word "paper." The long vowel "a" sound is located at the end of an open syllable. The "a" sound must be spelled using only "a." Therefore, "p-a-p-e-r" is the correct spelling. Based upon our understanding of the long vowel spelling process, we now know why the word "chain" must be spelled "c-h-ai-n." The long vowel "a" sound is in the middle of a one-syllable word. The same goes for words like "boat," "night," "feet," and "heat." Why are the words "sky," "way," "show," "flea," "due," and "dew" spelled the way that they are? If you said because the long vowel sound is located at the end of a one-syllable word, you are correct. The appropriate long vowel spelling must be used.

We're not out of the woods, yet, though. Note that in category 2, the v-e category, we are required to have a consonant after the long vowel sound. This means that the vowel sound is in the middle, but it is still a member of the v-e category. That means that the word will have two spellings: a v-e spelling and a middle of the word spelling. As we examine the spelling of the spoken word "tale," we hear that not only is there a consonant after the long vowel sound (placing it in category 2, v-e spelling), but also that the long vowel sound is located in the middle of a one-syllable word (placing it in category 3, middle spellings). By process, the spoken word "tale" can be spelled "t-a-l-e" and "t-ai-l." Both are legitimate spellings based upon the process, and both are words within their own right. The same may not be said, however, for "f-l-i-t-e" and "f-l-igh-t." Although both are legitimate spellings based upon the process, only "flight" is a real word. Unfortunately, the only way students will know which ones are real words and which ones just fit the process is through practice and exposure to literature. This same drill, however, can be applied to the other long vowel sounds to help students learn the long vowel spelling rules. You may wish to refer to the charts for each long vowel in Figure 19 for lists of words to use in this drill.

Rare Long Vowel Spellings

The long vowel spellings found in Figure 20 are rare. When the long vowel phoneme is needed in spelling, these should rarely be used. One such rare long vowel spelling is "ey," which is a long vowel spelling for the long "e" phoneme. It says / $\bar{e}$ / as in "money" (/ m / / $\breve{o}$ / / n / / $\bar{e}$ /). Some other examples include the words "kidney," "alley," "donkey," and "chimney."

The remaining rare long vowel spellings should be taught and reviewed so that students are aware of the phonogram and its pronunciation. More in-depth study should be pursued on an as-needed basis.

A full list of various words that can be used to teach the long vowel spellings to students can be found at http://www.prufrock.com/assets/clientpages/schoolsuccessdyslexia.aspx.

/ā/

open	v-e	middle	end
a	a-e	ai	ay
table	cape	rain	day
maple	date	pain	stay
bacon	pale	chain	way
Salem	skate	paint	slay
apex	tame	trait	play
agent	gate	train	pay

/ē/

open	v-e	middle/end	middle/end
e	e-e	ee	ea
recall	scheme	sheen	seat
legal	Pete	flee	sea
sequel	these	beet	beat
sequence	theme	sheet	lean
secret	scene	see	flea
refuse	eve	keep	clean

/ī/

open	v-e	middle	end
i	i-e	igh	y
tiger	kite	night	sky
pilot	like	knight	try
Midas	cite	right	by
pirate	nice	sight	my
tripod	ride	blight	fry
tirade	dime	fight	dry

/ō/

open	v-e	middle	end
o	o-e	oa	ow
pony	rope	boat	slow
mohawk	tone	cloak	glow
solar	lone	oath	grow
sonar	bone	loan	low
voter	phone	roam	sow
bonus	scope	foam	tow

Figure 19. Long vowel spelling examples.

/ū/			
open	**v-e**	**end**	**end**
u	u-e	ue	ew
pupil	rule	rescue	dew
ruler	mute	true	stew
tutor	cute	blue	new
stupid	cube	glue	knew
human	dune	sue	few
unit	fumes	rue	slew

Figure 19. Continued.

Syllable Types

There are seven types of syllables in the English language:

- open syllable,
- closed syllable,
- silent "e" syllable,
- vowel team (also called vowel digraph),
- consonant + "le" syllable,
- "r"-controlled syllable, and
- final stable syllables.

A full list of various words that can be used to teach the syllable types to students can be found at http://www.prufrock.com/assets/clientpages/schoolsuccessdyslexia.aspx.

Open Syllables

An open syllable is a syllable that ends with a vowel. They are primarily found in multisyllabic words. When a syllable ends in a vowel,

/ā/

middle spellings	middle spellings	end spellings	end spellings
ea	ei	eigh	ey
great	vein	weigh	they
steak	rein	sleigh	whey
break	skein	neigh	hey

/ē/

middle spellings	middle spellings	middle spellings	end spellings	end spellings
ie	ei	i	y	ey
piece	deceive	radio	bully	money
thief	receive	onion	city	valley

/ī/

one syllable spellings	end spellings
y-e	ie
type	pie
style	tie
hype	die

/ō/

end spellings
oe
doe
foe
toe

/ū/

middle spellings	middle spellings
eu	ui
feud	fruit
deuce	bruise
neuter	suit

Figure 20. Rare long vowel spellings.

the vowel is naturally long. For example, the word "total" has two syllables, "to" and "tal." The syllable "to" is the open syllable. Note that it ends with the vowel "o" and the vowel is long (/ t / / ō /). Notice the following open syllables (remember, the vowel at the end of the syllable is long):

- ve
- cu
- pri
- de
- fla
- ca
- to
- tri
- ma
- fri
- smu
- stre
- ja
- cla
- be
- re
- bri
- mu
- bro
- shri
- sho
- quo

Closed Syllables

A closed syllable is a syllable that ends with a consonant. When a syllable ends in a consonant, the vowel in the syllable is naturally short. For example, the word "vampire" has two syllables, "vam" and "pire." The syllable "vam" is the closed syllable. Note that the vowel in the syllable is short (/ v / / ă / / m /). Notice the following closed syllables (remember, the vowel in the middle of the syllable is short):

- blem
- riz
- zid
- vom
- bip
- vam
- dem
- yan
- lin
- deg
- but
- bez
- lon
- zond
- nult
- cul
- ket
- bot
- frip
- gog
- jan
- sud
- hig
- suf

Silent "e" Syllables

A silent "e" syllable is a syllable that ends with a silent "e." The purpose of the silent "e" at the end of the syllable is to make the vowel in the syllable long. For example, the word "confide" has two syllables, "con" and "fide." You will remember that the syllable "con" is closed because it ends with a consonant. However, the syllable "fide" is the silent "e" syllable because it ends with an "e" that is not pronounced. The sole purpose of the silent "e" is to make the "i" in the middle of the syllable long ($/ f / / \bar{\imath} / / d /$). Notice the following silent "e" syllables (remember, the "e" at the end of the syllable is silent, and the vowel in the middle of the syllable is long):

• dife	• nize	• bine	• tate
• yane	• habe	• bole	• mide
• fide	• fube	• hume	• ribe
• vuve	• tume	• vene	• vade
• fute	• yoke	• bose	• jate
• ite	• tude	• doke	

Vowel Team Syllables

A vowel team syllable is a syllable that contains any vowel digraph. Again, a digraph is two letters that work together to create one sound. In this case, a vowel digraph is two vowels that work together to create one sound, as in "ow" or "ay." The vowel team may end the syllable, creating what sounds like an open syllable, as in "feeble" (**fee** ble) or the vowel team may be followed by a consonant, as in "weapon" (**weap** on).

Students should have ample practice with vowel team syllables as they study the following vowel teams:

• ai	• igh	• ew	• ie
• ay	• oa	• ei	
• ee	• ow	• eigh	
• ea	• ue	• ey	

Consonant + "le" Syllables

A consonant + "le" syllable is a syllable that contains a consonant followed by "le," as in "wrinkle" or "wiggle." The "-kle" and the "-gle" in these words are consonant + "le" syllables. It is important to note that the vowel in the consonant + "le" syllable is not the "e" at the end. Instead, the vowel in the consonant + "le" syllable is implied, and the vowel has been reduced to a schwa. The schwa is the equivalent of the sound of a short "u," as in "cup" (/ *c* / / *ŭ* / / *p* /). The syllable "-kle," is pronounced / *k* / / *ə* / / *l* /. The syllable "-gle," is pronounced / *g* / / *ə* / / *l* /. To help identify consonant + "le" syllables, remember this: "Consonant + "le," count back three." [6] Notice the application and the location of consonant + "le" in the following words: "bubble," "riddle," "little," "boggle," "steeple," "whistle," "spectacle," "raffle," and "fizzle."

"R"-Controlled Syllables

An "r"-controlled syllable is a syllable that contains any form of the vowel + "r" formation. The vowel in an "r"-controlled syllable is immediately followed and controlled by an "r." The "r" seizes control of the syllable and distorts the sound of the vowel contained within the syllable. The "r," in essence, becomes the most prominent sound heard in the syllable. For example, the word "target" has two syllables, "tar" and "get." You will remember that the syllable "get" is closed because it ends with a consonant. However, the syllable "tar" is an "r"- controlled syllable. The "r" in "tar" seizes control of the entire syllable and distorts the short sound of the "a" in the closed syllable: / *t* / / *aw* / / *ər* /.

Vowel + "r" comes in three different forms:

- those that say / *aw* / / *ər* /, as in start (/ *s* / / *t* / / *aw* / / *ər* / / *t* /) and words like "barn," "barber," "chart," "smart," "farther," and "carpet";

---

6   Neither "-ckle" nor "-stle" follow the "count back three" mnemonic. In both cases, the syllable is divided after counting back four letters. In the case of the "-ckle," it is because the long spelling of the / k / phoneme is required. (See The Long Spelling Rule on p. 104). In the case of the "-stle," it is because the letter "t " in "-stle" is silent.

- those that say / ō / / er /, as in horn (/ h / / ō / / ər / / n /) and words like "north," "short," "born," "horse," "porch," "retort," "corner," and "normal"; and

- those that say / er /, as in her (/ h / / ər /). Because there are multiple forms of the "r"-controlled vowels that say / er /, we'll examine this form in more detail.

There are nine vowel + "r" forms that say / er /, as in her (/ h / / ər /):

- "er," as in "jerk," "copper," "swerve," "pattern," and "verse";

- "ir," as in "shirt," "birth," "girl," "thirst," and "confirm";

- "ur," as in "nurse," "murder," "churn," "disturb," and "surplus";

- "ar," as in "collar," "polar," "particular," "calendar," and "grammar";

- "ard," as in "lizard," "backward," "mustard," "custard," and "forward" (note that this will function as a final stable syllable in that it will appear at the end of a multisyllable word);

- "or," as in "instructor," "spectator," "ancestor," "worm," and "world" (note that "or" has two rules—it makes the / ər / sound when it's found at the end of words that refer to people when it follows a "t" or "s," and it appears after the letter "w");

- "ear," as in "earth," "search," "early," "hearse," and "earnest" (note that this is a rare spelling of the / ər / sound);

- "our," as in "flourish," "journey," and "nourish" (note that this is another rare spelling of the / ər / sound); and

- "yr," as in "martyr," "Myrtle," and "zephyr" (note that this is an extremely rare spelling of the / ər / sound).

Syllable Division

Syllable division is an important component in word attack skills. Word attack can best be described as applying the rules for decoding in order to properly identify the sequence of letters found in a word in preparation and correctly producing the phonemes found therein (pronunciation). Correct pronunciation is essential for pulling meaning from print. Let's demonstrate this by looking at a situation that you will see again momentarily. For example, let's take the word "camel." Our understanding of the concept present by the sequence of letters is directly proportional to our pronunciation of the sequence. We could pronounce the sequence as / k / / ā / / m / / ə / / l /. But, who has ever heard of a / k / / ā / / m / / ə / / l /? However, if we pronounce the sequence as / k / / ă / / m / / ə / / l /, we have an animal that we all have heard of.

Syllable division will be taught here in one of three ways.[7] Each of the three ways is appropriate based upon the construction of the multisyllabic word.

VC/CV (Vowel, Consonant, Consonant, Vowel) Division

When the multisyllabic word is of "vc/cv" construction, the word is divided into syllables by dividing between the two consonants. This means that the first syllable ends with a consonant and is a closed syllable. By definition, the vowel in the closed syllable is short. This is affectionately known as "rabbit division." Notice the application of "vc/cv" division in the following words:

- rabbit (rab/bit)
- tennis (ten/nis)
- plastic (plas/tic)
- nutmeg (nut/meg)
- insist (in/sist)
- spotter (spot/ter)

7   There exist two additional forms of syllable division that are not presented here: "v/v" and "vc/ccv" divisions.

- bobbin (bob/bin)
- sadden (sad/den)
- muffin (muf/fin)
- comment (com/ment)
- campus (cam/pus)
- dental (den/tal)

VCV Division #1

There are two types of "vcv" syllable division. In the first, affectionately known as "tiger division," we divide the word into syllables by dividing after the first vowel. This will make the first syllable an open syllable (v/cv) because it ends with a vowel. By definition, the vowel is long. Tiger division should always be your first choice when dividing a word of "vcv" construction. Notice the application of "v/cv" division in the following words:

- tiger (ti/ger)
- prevent (pre/vent)
- polite (po/lite)
- Venus (Ve/nus)
- rival (ri/val)
- unite (u/nite)
- direct (di/rect)
- bonus (bo/nus)
- behave (be/have)

VCV Division #2

The second form of "vcv" syllable division, affectionately called "camel division," is applied when the multisyllabic word is of "vcv" construction and "v/cv" or tiger division does not produce a recognizable word. In this case, we divide the word into syllables by dividing after the consonant (vc/v). This will make the first syllable a closed syllable. By definition, the vowel in a closed syllable must be short.

For example, let's divide the word "camel" into syllables. Following the rule for "vcv" syllable division, we would divide after the first vowel, the "a." Our syllable division would look like this: ca/mel. As mentioned previously, this would cause the first syllable to end with the vowel "a." This would make the vowel long. The word as we have divided it above would be pronounced $/ k / / \bar{a} / / m / / \partial / / l /$. But we know that is incorrect, so we close the first syllable by dividing after the consonant "m." Our division now looks like this: cam/el.

This changes the vowel from long to short: the "a" goes from / ā / to / ă /. The word is no longer pronounced as / k / / ā / / m / / ə / / l /, an animal that no one has heard of. It is now pronounced as / k / / ă / / m / / ə / / l /, an animal that we have all heard of.

Notice the application of "vc/v" division in the following words. In the first division following each word, remember that we must first try tiger division. This will not produce a recognizable word. So, we then close the first syllable and pronounce the word again. The second division following each word, camel division, will produce a recognizable word.[8]

- punish (pū/nish, pŭn/ish)
- second (sē/cond, sĕc/ond)
- grenade (grē/nade, grĕn/ade)
- wagon (wā/gon, wăg/on)
- panel (pā/nel, păn/el)
- salad (sā/lad, săl/ad)
- relic (rē/lic, rĕl/ic)
- abode (ā/bode, ăb/ode)
- rigid (rī/gid, rĭg/id)
- legend (lē/gend, lĕg/end)
- valid (vā/lid, văl/id)
- digit (dī/git, dĭg/it)
- colic (cō/lic, cŏl/ic)
- refuge (rē/fuge, rĕf/uge)

The Two Sounds of "oo"

The vowel team "oo" represents two sounds. It says / o͞o / as in tooth, and it says / o͝o / as in "good." It's used frequently in both forms, making it trickier than the other vowel teams. Unfortunately, there is no hard and fast rule to help with the differentiation of / o͞o / and / o͝o / when they appear in written form.

To generate the / o͞o / sound, as in "tooth," the lips are slightly rounded, and the tongue tip is at the base of the lower teeth. The

---

8   I have added the diacritics above the vowels in each of the first syllables to aid with understanding.

back of the tongue is high. A very small aperture is formed down the middle of the tongue. Voice is emitted through this aperture. Notice the application and the location of "oo" that says / *oo* / as in "tooth" in the following words: "broom," "food," "zoo," "hoop," "groove," "scoot," "mood," "loom," and "choose."

To generate the / *oo* / sound, as in "book," the lips should be slightly rounded. The jaw begins to open. The back of the tongue is relatively high. The front of the tongue is low, with the tongue tip at the base of the lower teeth as voice is emitted. Notice the application and the location of "oo" that says / *oo* / as in "book" in the following words: "shook," "wool," "foot," "crook," "wooden," and "cooker."

A full list of various words that can be used to teach the two sounds of "oo" to students can be found at http://www.prufrock.com/ assets/clientpages/schoolsuccessdyslexia.aspx.

The Two Sounds of "ou"

The vowel team "ou" represents two sounds: / *ou* / as in "mouth" and / *oo* / as in *soup*. Primarily, however, it's used to say / *ou* / as in "mouth." To generate this sound, one must understand that this sound is a hybrid of the / ŏ / and the / *oo* /. There is almost no elevation of the tongue during the generation of this sound. The mouth is open slightly. The lips are not as rounded, as for the / *aw* /, as the sound generated is shorter. After the / ŏ / has been generated, the jaw rises, and the lips remain rounded. A very small aperture is formed down the middle of the tongue, and / *oo* / is emitted through this aperture. Notice the application and the location of "ou" as in "mouth" in the following words: "mouse," "about," "around," "flour," "hound," "noun," "spout," "south," "cloud," "ouch," and "our."

The vowel team "ou" also says / *oo* / as in "soup." To generate this sound, the lips are slightly rounded, and the tongue tip is at the base of the lower teeth. The back of the tongue is high. A very small aperture is formed down the middle of the tongue. Voice is emitted through this aperture. Notice the application and the location of "ou" as in "soup" in the following words: "tour," "crouton," "you," "group," "coupon," "cougar," "contour," "caribou," and "acoustic."

A full list of various words that can be used to teach the two sounds of "ou" to students can be found at http://www.prufrock.com/assets/clientpages/schoolsuccessdyslexia.aspx.

The Two Sounds of "ow"

The vowel team "ow" represents two sounds. It can makes the long "o" phoneme, / ō /, as in "slow." Or it can say / ow /, as in "plow."

However, it primarily says / ō /, as in "slow." To generate this sound, remember that the phoneme / ō / is a diphthong or a vowel glide. A vowel glide begins as one sound and ends with another. To generate the / ō / diphthong, the elevation of the tongue is low, nearing the floor of the mouth. The lips are rounded. The mouth is slightly less open than for the short / ŏ /. The chin is at the second lowest position. After the generation of the initial phoneme, the lips contract as if to make the / w /. The change in mouth position generates the proper end to the / ō / phoneme. Notice the application and the location of "ow" as in "slow" in the following words: "mow," "stow," "flown," "window," "snow," "thrown," "willow," "growth," and "yellow."

The vowel team "ow" also says / ow / as in "plow." To generate this sound, remember that this sound is a hybrid of the / ŏ / and the / o͡o /. There is almost no elevation of the tongue during the generation of this sound. The mouth is open slightly. The lips are not as rounded as for the / aw /. The sound generated is shorter than for the / aw /. After the / ŏ / has been generated, the jaw rises, and the lips remain rounded. A very small aperture is formed down the middle of the tongue, and / o͡o / is emitted through this aperture. Notice the application and the location of "ow" as in "plow" in the following words: "howl," "clown," "towel," "brow," "town," "flower," and "how."

A full list of various words that can be used to teach the two sounds of "ow" to students can be found at http://www.prufrock.com/assets/clientpages/schoolsuccessdyslexia.aspx.

The Two Sounds of "c"

The consonant "c" generates two distinct sounds, called the soft (or unvoiced) "c" and the hard (or voiced) "c."

When followed by most letters, the letter "c" says / k /, as in "cut." This is called the hard "c." To generate the / k / phoneme, the tongue tip is at the base of the lower teeth. The back of the tongue rises to contact the soft palate (velum). Air pressure is released by the sudden dropping of the tongue. Notice the application of the hard "c" in the following words: "cape," "candle," "contest," "cake," "crow," "cook," "arctic," "curse," and "clip."

However, if the "c" is followed by an "e," "i," or "y," it says / s / as in "cent." This is called the soft "c." The rule applies even when the soft "c" doesn't begin a word, as in "space." To generate the / s / phoneme, the tongue is placed against the alveolar ridge. Air flows through a small aperture and out of the oral cavity, producing a hissing sound. Notice the application of the soft "c" as it is followed by an "e," "i," or "y" in the following words: "recite," "pencil," "dance," "city," "civil," "celery," "celebrate," "ice," "fancy," and "choice."

A full list of various words that can be used to teach the two sounds of "c" to students can be found at http://www.prufrock.com/assets/clientpages/schoolsuccessdyslexia.aspx.

The Two Sounds of "g"

Similar to the letter "c" the consonant "g" also generates two distinct sounds, called the soft (or unvoiced) "g" and the hard (or voiced) "g."

When followed by most letters, the letter "g" says / g /, as in "gun." This is called the hard "g." To generate the / g / phoneme, the tongue tip is at the base of the lower teeth. The back of the tongue rises to contact the soft palate (velum). Voice is added as air pressure is released by the sudden dropping of the tongue. Notice the application of the hard "g" in the following words: "grime," "goose," "glad," "grand," "gush," "gasp," "gore," "dog," "goggle," and "beggar."

However, if the "g" is followed by an "e," "i," or "y," it says / j /, as in "gem." This is called the soft "g." This rule applies even when the "g" is in the middle of a word, as in "cage." The phoneme / j / is articulated by raising the front part of the tongue to a point on the hard palate just behind the alveolar ridge. The lips are slightly rounded and the tongue is broadened along the alveolar ridge and touching molars on each side. Voice is added as air pressure is built up and exploded by suddenly dropping the tongue and the jaw. Notice the application of the soft "g" as it is followed by an "e," "i," or "y" in the following words: "clergy," "gist," "germ," "stooge," "wage," "German," "gentle," "lounge," and "village."

A full list of various words that can be used to teach the two sounds of "g" to students can be found at http://www.prufrock.com/assets/clientpages/schoolsuccessdyslexia.aspx.

The Two Sounds of "s"

Similar to the letters "c" and "g," the consonant "s" also generates two distinct sounds, called the soft (or unvoiced) "s" and the hard (or voiced) "s."

In most situations, the letter "s" is unvoiced or soft, as in "sun." To generate the / s / phoneme, the tongue is placed against the alveolar ridge. Air flows through a small aperture and out of the oral cavity, producing a hissing sound. Notice the application of the soft "s" in the following words: "bust," "slaps," "supper," "sort," "Sunday," "mask," "taps," "sand," "grasp," and "plastic."

However, when the "s" is located between two vowels, it says / z /, as in "nose," making it a hard "s." Further, when the "s" is at the end of a word and it follows a voiced sound, it says / z / as in "bugs," also a hard "s." Notice the application of the hard "s" in the following words[9]: "miser," "raise," "lies," "reason," "pose," "games," "hers," "surprise," "ease," and "his."

A full list of various words that can be used to teach the two sounds of "s" to students can be found at http://www.prufrock.com/assets/clientpages/schoolsuccessdyslexia.aspx.

The Three Sounds of "-ed"

The suffix "-ed" is a somewhat troublesome suffix, as it makes three different sounds based upon the consonant or sound that precedes it.

When the suffix "-ed" follows a "t " or a "d," it says / ĕd /[10] as in the following words: "granted," "pounded," "waited," "shouted," "plotted," and "nodded." When the suffix "-ed" follows a voiced sound, it says / d / as in the following words: "turned," "blazed," "fooled," "bloomed," "begged," and "snowed." Finally, when the suffix "-ed" follows an unvoiced sound, it says / t /, as in the following words: "jumped," "liked," "chased," "thanked," and "drooped."

---

9   Remember that all vowels are voiced. Vowel teams, as representatives of vowels, must also represent voiced sounds.

10 This has been reduced somewhat due to Americanized English. When Americans say the word "rented," we do not say "rent-ĕd." We say "rent-ĭd."

A full list of various words that can be used to teach the three sounds of "ed" to students can be found at http://www.prufrock.com/assets/clientpages/schoolsuccessdyslexia.aspx.

The Three Sounds of "ea"

The vowel team "ea" can be challenging, as it makes three different sounds.

First, "ea" says / ē /, as in "sea." As with other common long vowel spellings, the location of the phoneme in the pronunciation of the word is indicative of its spelling. In this case, "ea" is the normal spelling for a long "e" phoneme located in the middle or at the end of a word. Therefore, "ea" should be considered either a middle or an end spelling for a word with the long "e" phoneme. Notice the application of the "ea" phonogram as a long "e" phoneme in the following words: "seam," "beak," "meat," "treason," "breathe," and "gleam."

Second, "ea" says / ĕ /, as in "bed." Notice the application of "ea" as a short "e" phoneme in the following words: "spread," "threat," "heaven," "steady," "measure," "pleasant," and "feather."

Finally, "ea" says / ā /. There are three Anglo-Saxon base words where "ea" makes the long "a" phoneme: "great," "steak," and "break."

A full list of various words that can be used to teach the three sounds of "ea" to students can be found at http://www.prufrock.com/assets/clientpages/schoolsuccessdyslexia.aspx.

The Three Sounds of "y"

The letter "y" functions as both a consonant and a vowel. Therefore, it produces three sounds depending upon how it is used and where in the word it is located.

When "y" is used as a consonant, it appears at the beginning of a word or the beginning of a syllable. It makes the long "e" phoneme that is found in the word "feet," then it glides into the next sound made by the letter following the "y." Notice the application and the location of "y" as it says / ē / and then glides into the next sound in the following words: "yell," "yellow," "yak," "young," "yearling," "yeast," and "Yiddish."

When "y" is used as a vowel, it has two primary sounds. First, when "y" is at the end of a one-syllable word, "y" says / ī /, as found in the word "bike." Notice the location and application of "y" that says / ī / at the end of the following one-syllable words: "dry," "sly," "my," "sky," "sty," and "why."

When "y" is at the end of a multisyllabic word, it primarily says / ē /, as in "lady," "bunny," "baby," "truly," "cemetery," "crazy," "elementary," "needy," and "mostly."

A full list of various words that can be used to teach the three sounds of "y" to students can be found at http://www.prufrock.com/assets/clientpages/schoolsuccessdyslexia.aspx.

"au" Versus "aw"

Both "au" and "aw" say / aw /, as in "saw" or "haul." However, they may not be used interchangeably.

Students should use "au" when the / aw / phoneme is at the beginning or in the middle of a word. Therefore, it is viewed as a beginning or middle spelling. To generate the / aw / phoneme, the elevation of the tongue is low, nearing the floor of the mouth. The lips are rounded. The mouth is slightly more open than for the short / oo /. The chin is at the lowest possible position as voice is emitted. Notice the application of this rule and the location of the "au" as it says / aw / in the following words: "August," "autumn," "sauce," "launch," "fauna," "fraud," "caucus," "launder," and "haunt."

Students should use "aw" when the / *aw* / phoneme comes at the end of the word or when the / *aw* / phoneme is located directly in front of an "1 " or "n." It is primarily viewed as an end spelling. Notice the application of this rule in the following words: "yawn," "shawl," "draw," and "straw."

A full list of various words that can be used to teach the sounds of "au" and "aw" to students can be found at http://www.prufrock.com/assets/clientpages/schoolsuccessdyslexia.aspx.

"ie" Versus "ei"

The vowel teams "ie" and "ei" represent a very unique situation in the English code. They make the same sound, / *ē* /, as in "thief" or "deceit," and their spellings are easily confused.

The vowel team "ie" primarily says / *ē* /, as in "thief." It is a rare middle spelling for the long "e" phoneme. Notice the application of "ie" as it says / *ē* / in the following words: "priest," "wield," "believe," "relief," "diesel," and "niece."

After the letter "c," the vowel team "ie" is spelled "ei, " and it says / *ē* /, as in "receive," "conceit," "receipt," "deceive," "ceiling," and "perceive."

A full list of various words that can be used to teach the sounds of "ie" and "ei" to students can be found at http://www.prufrock.com/assets/clientpages/schoolsuccessdyslexia.aspx.

"oi" Versus "oy"

Both "oi" and "oy" say / *ō* / / *ē* /, as in "boil" or "boy." However, they may not be used interchangeably.

Use "oi" when the / ō / / ē / phoneme is at the beginning or in the middle of a word. Therefore, it is viewed as a beginning or middle spelling. Notice the application of this rule and the location of "oi" as it says / ō / / ē / in the following words: "coil," "hoist," "devoid," "exploit," "sirloin," "choice," "poison," "turmoil," and "ointment."

Students should use "oy" when the / ō / / ē / phoneme comes at the end of the word. It is primarily viewed as an end spelling. Notice the application of this rule and the location of the / ō / / ē / phoneme in the following words: "decoy," "alloy," "soy," "enjoy," "employ," and "convoy."

A full list of various words that can be used to teach the sounds of "oi" and "oy" to students can be found at http://www.prufrock.com/assets/clientpages/schoolsuccessdyslexia.aspx.

"ou" Versus "ow"

Both "ou" and "ow" say / ŏ / / oo /, as in "foul" or "now." However, they may not be used interchangeably.

Students should use "ou" when the / ŏ / / oo / phoneme is in the beginning or the middle of a word. Therefore, it is viewed as a beginning or middle spelling. Notice the application and the location of "ou" that says (/ ŏ / / oo /) in the following words: "mouse," "about," "flour," "pound," and "couch."

Students should use "ow" when the / ŏ / / oo / phoneme comes at the end of the word, when the / ŏ / / oo / phoneme is located directly in front of an "l" or "n," or if the / ŏ / / oo / phoneme is followed by "-er" or "-el." It is primarily viewed as an end spelling. Notice the application and the location of "ow" that says / ŏ / / oo / in the following words: "scowl," "towel," "brow," "town," and "flower."

A full list of various words that can be used to teach the sounds of "ou" and "ow" to students can be found at http://www.prufrock.com/assets/clientpages/schoolsuccessdyslexia.aspx.

"qu"

The "q" represents another unique situation in the English code. The "q" never appears in our language without a "u" immediately following it. Although the letter "u" is a vowel, it functions in this case as part of a consonant blend, and it says / w /. For the blend "qu," we say / k / and immediately follow the / k / sound with the / w / sound: / k / / w /. Notice the application of "qu" in the following words: "quiz," "quotient," "quick," "square," "quaint," "quench," "require," and "aquatic."

A full list of various words that can be used to teach "qu" to students can be found at http://www.prufrock.com/assets/clientpages/schoolsuccessdyslexia.aspx.

"-ald," "-alk," "-all," "-alt," "-ild," "-ind," "-old," "-oll," "-olt," and "-ost"

The vowel-consonant-consonant construction in single-syllable words presents a unique opportunity in the English code, for the "vcc" construction can be classified in three categories: "a"-consonant-consonant, "i"-consonant-consonant, and "o"-consonant-consonant.

The vowel in the "a"-consonant-consonant construction is pronounced as / aw /, like the / aw / in "haul" or "hawk." The pattern "a"-consonant-consonant appears in four forms: "-ald," "-alk,"[11] "-all," and "-alt." Notice the application and the location of "a"-consonant-consonant as the vowel "a" says / aw / in the following words: "scald," "talk," "ball," "halt," "waltz," "stalk," and "squall."

The vowel in the "i"-consonant-consonant construction is pronounced as / $\bar{\imath}$ /, like in "kite." The pattern "i"-consonant-consonant appears in two forms: "-ild " and "-ind "[12]. Notice the application and

---

11   The -alk phonogram is pronounced / aw / / k /. We say "talk" (/ t / / aw / / k /). For -ald, -all, and -alt, the "l" is pronounced.

12   The "i" in the word "wind" is long only when the word represents a verb (/ w / / $\bar{\imath}$ / / n / / d /). When it is a noun, the "i" is short (/ w / / i / / n / / d /).

the location of "i"-consonant-consonant as the vowel "i" says / ī / in the following words: "child," "kind," "mild," and "rewind."

The vowel in the "o"-consonant-consonant construction is pronounced as / ō /, like in "bone." The pattern "o"-consonant-consonant appears in five forms: "-old," "-olk," [13] "-oll," "-olt," and "-ost." Notice the application and the location of "o"-consonant-consonant as the vowel "o" says / ō / in the following words: "scold," "roll," "bolt," "most," and "folk."

A full list of various words that can be used to teach the vowel-consonant-consonant spellings to students can be found at http://www.prufrock.com/assets/clientpages/schoolsuccessdyslexia.aspx.

Silent Letters

There are many words in the English code that present a unique spelling challenge. These are words that contain a silent letter. Silent letters present a challenge because they are not pronounced and therefore are easily forgotten when spelled.

The following list is not comprehensive. I would caution the teacher or parent against teaching any of the following words without the student having demonstrated a need for them. If, however, you find it necessary, I would suggest teaching these words as Anglo-Saxon sight words. The following words contain silent letters:

- **silent "b"**: "bomb," "dumb," "tomb," "crumb," "debt," "doubt," "comb," "thumb"

- **silent "c"**: "scene," "scent," "science," "scissors," "scythe," "abscess," "czar," "scepter"

- **silent "g"**: "malign," "sign," "design," "assignment," "assign," "reign," "gnaw," "gnome"

---

13   The -olk phonogram is pronounced / ō / / k /. We say "folk" (/ f / / ō / / k /) and "yolk" (/ ē / / ō / / k /). For -old, -oll, -ost, and -olt, the "l" or "s" is pronounced.

- **silent "h":** "rhinoceros," "ghastly," "afghan," "exhibit," "ghost," "exhaust," "spaghetti," "rhubarb"

- **silent "k":** "knee," "known," "knife," "knock"

- **silent "l":** "calf," "half," "calves," "halves"

- **silent "n":** "condemn," "hymn," "column," "autumn," "solemn"

- **silent "p":** "receipt," "raspberry," "corps," "cupboard," "psychiatry," "psychology," "pseudonym," "pneumonia"

- **silent "s":** "aisle," "isle," "island"

- **silent "t":** "moisten," "glisten," "listen," "soften," "often," "fasten," "christen"

- **silent "u":** "buy," "build," "built," "guess," "guard," "guilt," "guitar," "guarantee"

- **silent "w":** "sword," "answer," "wreck," "wrote," "wreak," "wrong," "wrist," "wrap"

A full list of various words that can be used to teach the silent letters to students can be found at http://www.prufrock.com/assets/clientpages/schoolsuccessdyslexia.aspx.

The Long Spelling Rule

The long spelling rule involves six different phonograms. However, the six phonograms represent three pairs that are very similar: "-ch"/"-tch," "-k"/ "-ck," and "-g"/ "-dge". Both the "-ch" and the "-tch" make the / *ch* / sound. The "-k" and the -ck make the / *k* / sound. The "-g" and "-dge" both make the / *j* / sound. The long spelling rule tells us when to use which half of each pair.

- **"-ch" versus "-tch":** Use the "-*ch*" when the / *ch* / phoneme is needed, as in "lunch," "crunch," "wrench," "pinch," and "branch." However, when the / *ch* / phoneme comes *imme-*

diately after a short vowel, the longer / *ch* / spelling, "-tch," is used, as in "stitch," "batch," "clutch," "fetch," and "kitchen."

- **"-g" versus "-dge"**: Use the "-g" when the / *j* / phoneme is needed in the middle or end of a word, as in "lunge," "cringe," "large," and "range." However, when the / *j* / phoneme comes *immediately* after a short vowel, the longer / *j* / spelling, "-dge," is used, as in "trudge," "ridge," "badge," "sledge," "dodge," and "judge."

- **"-k" versus "-ck"**: Use the "-k" when the / *k* / phoneme is needed in the middle or end of a word, as in "brink," "trunk," "rank," and "blanket." However, when the / *k* / phoneme comes *immediately* after a short vowel, the longer / *k* / spelling, "-ck," is used, as in "clock," "lack," "truck," "deck," "pluck," and "flick."

A full list of various words that can be used to teach the long spelling rules to students can be found at http://www.prufrock.com/assets/clientpages/schoolsuccessdyslexia.aspx.

The "f," "l," "s" Doubling Rule

The "f," "l," "s" doubling rule is a spelling rule that states that when an "f," "l," or "s" immediately follows a short vowel, the "f," "l," or "s" must be doubled. When most consonants immediately follow a short vowel, the single consonant is all that is required, as in "whim," "wet," and "hid."

Note that all three of the words contain a short vowel. Yet, only one consonant is found immediately following the short vowel. However, in the following examples, the "f," "l," "s" doubling rule is applied because the "f," "l," and "s" come *immediately* after the short vowel: "whiff," "well," and "hiss." Here are further examples of the "f," "l," "s" doubling rule: "stress," "huff," "grill," "staff," "dress," and "thrill."

A full list of various words that can be used to teach the "f," "l," "s" doubling rule to students can be found at http://www.prufrock.com/ assets/clientpages/schoolsuccessdyslexia.aspx.

The CVC Doubling Rule

The cvc doubling rule is a spelling rule that states that when a one-syllable word ends in a consonant-vowel-consonant construction (cvc), the last consonant is doubled before a vowel suffix is added.

Notice the application of the cvc doubling rule in the following words:

- split + ing = splitting
- trim + ed = trimmed
- rob + er = robber

In the examples above, the words "split," "trim," and "rob" all end with a consonant-vowel-consonant construction. The suffixes being added to them, "-ing," "-ed," and "-er," are all vowel suffixes because the first letter in the suffix is a vowel. In each example, the last consonant has been doubled when attaching the vowel suffix. Here are further examples of the cvc doubling rule: "barred," "druggist," "rotten," "whipped," "slimmer," and "quitting."

The cvc doubling rule *does not* apply when adding a consonant suffix to one-syllable-words that end with consonant-vowel-consonant construction: sad + ness = sadness.

Note that in the example above, the word "sad" has a consonant-vowel-consonant construction. The suffix being added to it, "-ness," is not a vowel suffix because the first letter in the suffix is a consonant. It is a consonant suffix. Therefore, the last consonant in "sad" has not been doubled before attaching the suffix.

A full list of various words that can be used to teach the cvc doubling rule to students can be found at http://www.prufrock.com/assets/clientpages/schoolsuccessdyslexia.aspx.

The Silent "e" Rule

The silent "e" rule is a spelling rule that covers the addition of suffixes to words that end with a silent "e." When a vowel suffix is added to a word that ends with a silent "e," the "e" is dropped before adding the vowel suffix. Notice the application of the silent "e" rule in the following words:

- create + ive = creative
- nerve + ous = nervous
- carve + ing = carving
- noise + y = noisy
- score + ed = scored
- note + able = notable

When a consonant suffix is added to a word that ends with a silent "e," the "e" is *not* dropped before adding the consonant suffix. Notice the application of the silent "e" rule in the following words:

- waste + ful = wasteful
- like + ness = likeness
- engage + ment = engagement
- lone + ly = lonely
- home + less = homeless

When adding the vowel suffixes "-able" or "-ous" to words that end in "-ce" or "-ge," the silent "e" is *not* dropped so that the "c" or "g" remains soft. Notice the exception to the silent "e" rule in the following words:

- enforce + able = enforceable

- courage + ous = courageous

- service + able = serviceable

- outrage + ous = outrageous

When adding vowel suffixes to words that end in "-ee," the silent "e" is not dropped.

Notice the exception to the silent "e" rule in the following words:

- see + ing = seeing

- agree + able = agreeable

The "y" Rule

The "y" rule is a spelling rule that covers the addition of suffixes to words that end with a "y." The rule hinges upon the letter that appears immediately before the "y."

When the letter before the "y" is a vowel, keep the "y" when adding the suffix, as in the following words:

- stay + ing = staying

- employ + er = employer

- annoy + ance = annoyance

- boy + ish = boyish

- journey + ed = journeyed

- convey + ance = conveyance

When the letter before the "y" is a consonant, change the "y" to "i" before adding a suffix, as in the following words:

- rely + able = reliable
- supply + er = supplier
- bury + ed = buried
- comply + ance = compliance
- library + an = librarian
- marry + age = marriage
- luxury + ous = luxurious

When the letter before the "y" is a consonant *and* the suffix begins with "i," keep the "y," as in the following words:

- study + ing = studying
- spy + ing = spying
- copy + ing = copying

Final Stable Syllables

Final stable syllables are literally what the name implies: They are syllables that occur at the end of words with more than one syllable (multisyllabic), and their representation is consistent. For example, the final stable syllable "-age" (pronounced / ĭ / / j /) always appears at the end of a multisyllabic word. The same goes for "-tion," "-ible," and "-ment."

Following is a comprehensive list of final stable syllables. Some are of Latinate origin, some are of Anglo-Saxon origin, and others are of French origin. Although I have addressed Anglo-Saxon, Latinate, and French word construction elsewhere in this work, I have chosen to include the suffixes (final stable syllables) and their meanings here.

- **"-able" (capable of; fit for):** The final stable syllable "-able" says / ə / / b / / ə / / l / and creates an adjective, as in the following words: "variable," "justifiable," "preferable," "applicable," and "livable."

- **"-age" (action; result of an action):** The final stable syllable "-age" says / ĭ / / j / and creates a noun or an adjective, as in the following words: "message," "average," "cottage," "salvage," and "package."

- **"-al" (relating to; characterized by):** The final stable syllable "-al" says / ə / / l / and creates an adjective or a noun, as in the following words: "abnormal," "original," "accidental," "legal," and "personal."

- **"-ain" (performing an action; result of an action):** The final stable syllable "-ain" says / ĭ / / n / and creates a verb, noun, or adverb ("again"), as in the following words: "bargain," "curtain," "captain," "porcelain," and "mountain."

- **"-ance" (action; state or condition):** The final stable syllable "-ance" primarily says / ə / / n / / s / and creates a noun or an adjective, as in the following words: "entrance," "resistance," "dominance," "performance," and "defiance."

- **ant" (performing an action; being in a condition):** The final stable syllable "-ant" says / ə / / n / / t / and creates a noun or an adjective, as in the following words: "tolerant," "blatant," "hesitant," "relevant," and "dominant."

- **"-ary" (of or relating to):** The final stable syllable "-ary" says / ĕ / / ər / / ē / and creates a noun or an adjective, as in the following words: "arbitrary," "visionary," "momentary," "primary," "customary," and "secondary." Occasionally, the final stable syllable "-ary" says / ər / / ē / as in the following words: "rotary," "glossary," "elementary," "summary," and "quandary."

- **"-ate" (having; characterized by):** The final stable syllable "-ate" says / ā / / t / and creates a verb, as in the following words: "separate," "duplicate," "translate," "associate," and "evacuate." Occasionally, the final stable syllable "-ate" says / ĭ / / t / and creates an adjective or a noun, as in the following words: "separate," "certificate," "considerate," "duplicate," and "climate."

- **"-cial" (relating to; characterized by):** The final stable syllable "-cial" says / sh / / ə / / l / and creates an adjective or a noun, as in the following words: "superficial," "crucial," "artificial," "unofficial," and "glacial." When the final stable syllable "-cial" follows an "n," it says / ch / / ə / / l / and creates an adjective, as in the following words: "financial" and "provincial."

- **"-cian" (someone who specializes in):** The final stable syllable "-cian" says / sh / / ə / / n / and always creates a noun, as in the following words: "magician," "mortician," "politician," "electrician," and "physician."

- **"-cious" (relating to; characterized by):** The final stable syllable "-cious" says / sh / / ə / / s / and creates an adjective, as in the following words: "spacious," "ferocious," "voracious," "gracious," and "atrocious."

- **"-el" (relating to; characterized by):** The final stable syllable "-el " says / ə / / l / and creates an adjective or a noun, as in the following words: "apparel," "sequel," "damsel," "tunnel," and "flannel."

- **"-ence" (performing a particular action):** The final stable syllable "-ence" says / ə / / n / / s / and creates a noun, as in the following words: "convenience," "sentence," "intelligence," "persistence," and "deference."

- **"-ery" (state or condition):** The final stable syllable "-ery" says / ər / / ē / and creates an adjective or a noun, as in the following words: "mystery," "grocery," "refinery," "flattery," "artillery." In one rare exception, the word "cemetery," the final stable syllable "-ery" says / ĕ / / ər / / ē /. In this condition, the final stable syllable creates a noun.

- **"-ible" (capable of; fit for):** The final stable syllable "-ible" says / ĭ / / b / / ə / / / l / and creates an adjective, as in the following words: "horrible," "impossible," "visible," "negligible," and "tangible."

- **"-ic" (of or relating to, having the nature of):** The final stable syllable "-ic" says / ĭ / / k / and creates a noun or an adjective, as in the following words: "magic," "electric," "critic," "citric," and "clinic."

- **"-ical" (of or relating to, having the nature of):** The final stable syllable "-ical " says / ĭ / / k / / ə / / / l / and creates an adjective, as in the following words: "magical," "electrical," "critical," "identical," and "clinical."

- **"-ically" (of or relating to; having the nature of):** The final stable syllable "-ically" says / ĭ / / k / / ə / / / l / / ē / and creates an adjective or an adverb, as in the following words: "magically," "electrically," "critically," "chronologically," " and "clinically."

- **"-ing" (performing an action; being in a condition):** The final stable syllable "-ing" says / ē / / ng / and creates a gerund or the present participle form of a verb, as in the following words: "walking," "parking," "considering," "carrying," and "liking."

- **"-ity" (relating to, made of):** The final stable syllable "-ity" says / ĭ / / t / / ē / and creates a noun or an adjective, as in the following words: "activity," "adversity," "brutality," "versatility," and "capacity."

- **"-less" (without; lacking; unable to be):** The final stable syllable "-less" says / l / / ĕ / / s / and creates an adjective, as in the following words: "thoughtless," "careless," "harmless," "pitiless," and "artless."

- **"-ly" (having the characteristics of):** The final stable syllable "-ly" says / l / / ē / and creates an adverb, as in the following words: "likely," "hourly," "bravely," "really," and "madly."

- **"-ness" (state; condition; quality):** The final stable syllable "-ness" says / n / / ĕ / / s / and creates a noun, as in the following words: "brightness," "goodness," "darkness," "likeness," and "lifelessness."

- **"-ory" (of; relating to):** The final stable syllable "-ory" says / ō / / ər / / ē / and creates a noun or an adjective, as in the following words: "auditory," "victory," "inventory," "promissory," and "preparatory." Additionally, the final stable syllable "-ory" says / ər / / ē / and creates a noun or an adjective, as in the following words: "factory," "accessory," "cursory," "contradictory," and "sensory."

- **"-ous" (full of; having the qualities of):** The final stable syllable "-ous" says / ə / / s / and creates an adjective, as in the following words: "marvelous," "fabulous," "dangerous," "slanderous," and "tremendous."

- **"-sion" (action or process; result):** The final stable syllable "-sion" says / sh / / ə / / n / and creates a noun, as in the following words: "propulsion," "mission," "permission," "session," and "omission." When the final stable syllable "-sion" follows an "r" or a vowel, it says / zh / / ə / / n / and creates a noun, as in the following words: "version," "invasion," "confusion," "adhesion," and "decision."

- **"-tial" (relating to; characterized by):** The final stable syllable "-tial" says / sh / / ə / / l / and creates an adjective or a noun, as in the following words: "spatial," "initial," "martial," "nuptial," and "impartial." When the final stable syllable "-tial" follows an "n" or an "s," it says / ch / / ə / / l / and creates an adjective, as in the following words: "substantial," "residential," "credential," "celestial," and "bestial."

- **"-tion" (action or process; result):** The final stable syllable "-tion" says / sh / / ə / / n / and creates a noun, as in the following words: "fiction," "temptation," "auction," "infraction," and "conception." When the final stable syllable "-tion" follows an "n" or an "s," it says / ch / / ə / / n / and still creates a noun, as in the following words: "question," "digestion," "suggestion," "attention," and "prevention."

A full list of various words that can be used to teach the final stable syllables to students can be found at http://www.prufrock.com/assets/clientpages/schoolsuccessdyslexia.aspx.

The Accent

In the English code, "accent" refers to how a syllable is stressed or emphasized during the decoding or reading process. A syllable that is accented receives a sharper, highlighted pronunciation from the other syllables in the word. Accented syllables:

- are pronounced more loudly than the other syllables in the word,
- receive a more forceful tone than the other syllables in the word,
- receive a slightly higher pitch than the other syllables in the word, and
- are part of every multisyllabic word (words with more than one syllable). For example, the word "catfish" is a multisyllabic word. It has more than one syllable, and one of the syllables is an accented syllable. It can be divided into syllables by using the "vccv" division rule.

All syllables that are accented in the English code are designated by a mark called the accent mark, which looks like this: '. The mark is placed above and to the right of the last letter in the accented syllable. Pronounce the word "catfish," and see if you can identify the accented syllable. If you said the first syllable, you're correct! When the accent mark is applied, the word looks like the following: cat'fish.

There are some basic rules for accents, including:

- In a two-syllable Anglo-Saxon compound word, the accent is on the first syllable: "sail'boat"

- In a Latinate word with a root and a suffix, the accent is on the root: "struc'ture"

- In a Latinate word with a root and a prefix, the accent is on the root: "ad vance'"

- Occasionally, in a Latinate word with a root and a prefix, the accent is on the prefix: "con'tact"

- In a word with a Greek combining form and a suffix or a base word and a suffix, the accent is on the combining form or the base word: "therm'al" or "base'ment"

- In a Latinate word with a prefix, root, and suffix, the accent is generally on the root: "ap par'ent"

- In a Latinate word ending with the suffix "-sion," "-tion," or "-cian," the accent is on the syllable that immediately precedes the suffix: "dis lo ca'tion" or "com pul'sion"

- In a multisyllabic word that ends with a silent "e" suffix, count back three syllables to find the one with the accent: "ac com' mod ate" or "in'com plete" or "e rad'ic ate"

The Schwa

The schwa is a phoneme that is produced when the vowel sound has been reduced. By reduction, the vowel sound appears in an unaccented syllable, as / ŭ / as in "hut." Regardless if the vowel is an "a", "e," "i," "o," "u," or "y," it may be reduced to a schwa if it appears in an unaccented syllable. When the vowel is reduced to a schwa, it is identified by the phonetic symbol / ə /.

For example, take the word "kitchen." To divide the word into syllables, we merely divide after the "h." This gives us two syllables, *kitch*

+ *en*. It looks like the following once the accent mark has been applied: "kitch'en"

The second syllable, "-en," is clearly unaccented. As a closed syllable, the vowel in "-en" should say / ĕ / as in "egg." Yet, we do not say / k / / ĭ / / ch / '/ ĕ / / n/. The "e" in the second syllable has been reduced to a schwa. The proper pronunciation is / k / / ĭ / / ch / '/ ə / / n /. The vowel "e" sounds like the / ŭ / as in "hut." Notice the schwa as it says / e / in the following words:

- wagon: / w / / ă / / g / '/ ə / / n /
- complete: / k / / ə / / m / / p / / l / / ē / / t /'

Plurals

A word that is plural indicates more than one. In the English code, we have been taught that words are made plural by simply adding an "-s." This seems to be a logical step; however, there is more involved in the process of making words in the English code plural. The English language represents a myriad of other languages, and each language has rules that govern its application. The following rules should serve as guidelines for making words in the English code plural:

- The majority of words are made plural by simply adding an "-s." For example, "table" becomes "tables" and "mind" becomes "minds."

- Words that end with the letter "y" have two forms. If there is a vowel immediately before the "y," keep the "y" and add an "-s." For example, "toy" becomes "toys" and "bay" becomes "bays." If there is a consonant immediately before the "y," change the "y" to "i," and then add "-es." For example, "baby" becomes "babies" and "navy" becomes "navies."

- Words that end with the letter "o" have two forms. If there is a vowel immediately before the "o," simply add an "-s." For example, "shampoo" becomes "shampoos" and "radio" becomes "radios." If there is a consonant immediately before the "o," add "-es." For example, "tomato" becomes "tomatoes" and "potato" becomes "potatoes."

- Words that end with "-s," "-x," "-ch," "-sh," or "-tch" are made plural by adding "-es." For example, "batch" becomes "batches," "dish" becomes "dishes," and "box" becomes "boxes."

- Words that end with "-f" or "-fe" generally are made plural by changing the "-f" or "-fe" to "-v" and adding "-es." For example, "knife" becomes "knives" and "elf" becomes "elves."

- The following nouns are made plural by a more radical change in the spelling of the word. Unfortunately, there is no spelling rule that governs the changes in the following words. Therefore, it would serve students to memorize the list:
  - "child" becomes "children"
  - "ox" becomes "oxen"
  - "goose" becomes "geese"
  - "man" becomes "men"
  - "woman" becomes "women"
  - "mouse" becomes "mice"
  - "foot" becomes "feet"
  - "tooth" becomes "teeth"
  - "louse" becomes "lice"

- Finally, there exists a group of nouns that are made plural by no change whatsoever in the spelling of the word. Unfortunately, there is no spelling rule that governs the lack of changes in the following words.
  - "sheep" stays as "sheep"
  - "grapefruit" stays as "grapefruit"
  - "fish" stays as "fish"

- ○ "moose" stays as "moose"
- ○ "salmon" stays as "salmon"
- ○ "pants" stays as "pants"
- ○ "deer" stays as "deer"
- ○ "species" stays as "species"

Chapter Summary

The 44 sounds in the English language and the rules that govern them help us with the sound/symbol correspondence that the National Reading Panel (Learning Points Associates, 2004) noted is so vital to the skill set of burgeoning readers. One area that remains to be covered and added to this skill set is morphology. Let's look at how the English language is constructed in the next chapter.

chapter 5

English Language Word Construction

T H E English language, like many of the approximately 2,700 spoken and written languages in the world, is composed of a mixture of other linguistic influences. Specifically, the linguistic influences upon English come in the form of how we construct the words that compose our spoken and written language. The three main linguistic models of word construction that constitute the English language are:

- Latinate word construction (55%),
- Anglo-Saxon word construction (25%), and
- Greek word construction (11%).

A little more than one out of every two words in our language is based upon Latinate word construction. One out of every four words in our language is based upon Anglo-Saxon word construction; however, please note that Anglo-Saxon word construction occupies nearly 100% of all words learned through the third grade. As a result, knowledge of Anglo-Saxon word construction forms a critical foundation for reading and spelling the English language. Finally, a little more than one out of every 10 words in our language is based upon Greek word construction. It bears mentioning, though, that most of the advanced vocabulary from mathematics and the sciences are based upon Greek word construction. Additionally, there are vocabulary words from math and the sciences that are hybrids between Greek word construction and Latinate word construction.

Latinate Word Construction

Studying Latinate word construction is not only a worthwhile endeavor, it is crucial to the academic foundation of students. By studying Latinate word construction, a struggling reader will improve her:

- vocabulary skills,

- word recognition skills (visual imagery), and

- word attack (decoding or reading) skills.

Students will first encounter Latinate word construction in approximately the fourth grade, and they will see it for the rest of their academic careers. In order for students who are struggling with language acquisition to be successful, these students will need remediation in Latinate roots, prefixes, suffixes, and connectives. These are four components that may play a role in the construction of a Latinate word.

- **Prefix:** A prefix is a letter or phonogram that is added to the beginning of a root. The addition of a prefix changes the meaning of the root because prefixes indicate, most frequently, the direction of the action. For example, take a look at the word "erupt." The word is composed of two parts: the prefix "e" and the root "rupt." The root "rupt" means "to break." The prefix "e" (from the assimilated prefix "ex-") means "out." So, "to erupt" means "to break out."

- **Root:** The root is a word part to which affixes (prefixes and suffixes) are added in order to create words. In the previous example, the prefix "e" was added to the Latinate root "rupt" to create the word "erupt." We need not add a prefix to our root to create a word. We may also add a suffix. For example, take the word "rupture." The word is composed of two parts: the root "rupt" and the suffix "ture."

- **Latinate connective:** The Latinate connective is used to connect the Latinate root to a suffix. For example, take the word "congratulate." The word is composed of four parts: a prefix ("con-"), a root ("grat"), a Latinate connective ("ul"), and a suffix ("-ate"). There are four Latinate connectives: "i," "ol," "u," and "ul."[14]

- **Suffix:** A suffix is a letter or phonogram that is added to the end of a root. The addition of a suffix changes the tense or part of speech of the root. (See the example for "rupture," above.)

Latinate word construction may appear in five basic forms[15]:

- **Prefix + root:** Take the Latinate prefix "re-" which means "back or again." Add the Latinate root "port," which means "to carry." Combine them, and you get the word "report," which means "to carry back."

- **Root + suffix:** Take the Latinate root "mot," which means "to move." Add the Latinate suffix "-tion," which means "the result of an action." Combine them, and you get the word "motion," which means "the result of moving."

- **Prefix + root + suffix:** Take the Latinate prefix "trans-," which means "across." Add the Latinate root "mis," which means "to

---

14 Most academic language therapists do not teach "ol" as a connective, as it rarely occurs.

15 There exist other combinations that are more advanced. For example, the word "disproportionate" has two prefixes, the Latinate prefixes "dis-" and "pro-," as well as two suffixes, the Latinate suffixes "-tion" and "-ate."

send." Then add the Latinate suffix "-sion," which means "the result of an action." Combine them, and you get the word "transmission," which means "the result of sending across."

- **Prefix + root + connective + suffix:** Take the Latinate prefix "ir-," a form of the assimilated Latinate prefix "in-," which means "in," "no," or "not." Here, it means "not." Add the Latinate root "reg," which means "straight." Then add the connective "ul." Lastly, add the suffix "-ar," which means "that which is." Combine them, and you get the word "irregular," which means "that which is not straight."

- **Root + connective + suffix:** Take the Latinate root "grad," which means "to step." Add the connective "u." Then add the Latinate suffix "-al," which means "characterized by." Combine them, and you get the word "gradual," which means "characterized by a step."

The most critical component of Latinate word construction is the Latinate root. The meaning of any word that contains a Latinate root must revolve around the meaning or concept of the root. Better stated, if a student can identify a Latinate root within a word *and* the root's meaning, the student has foundational knowledge of the meaning around which the word revolves.

Let's go back to our very first example of Latinate word construction, "prefix" + "root." We combined the prefix "re-"with the root "port" and created the word "report." Our task here is to focus on the Latinate root "port," which means "to carry." The meaning of any word that has the Latinate root "port" must revolve around the concept of "to carry," as in:

- im**port**
- trans**port**ation
- dispro**port**ionate
- op**port**unity
- insup**port**able

Each of the aforementioned words has the same Latinate root, "port." By definition, the meaning of each of the aforementioned words must revolve around the concept of "to carry."

Studying Latinate roots is an ideal vocabulary building exercise. In the curriculum I use, 150 Latinate roots are taught. Each root is used in approximately 50–350 words. When I work with a student on vocabulary, I always give him an option: I tell him that he can either memorize the definitions of 50 words, or he can remember one root. Invariably, students choose the root.

Identifying Words of Latinate Origin

Words of Latinate origin, like those of Anglo-Saxon and Greek origins, are easy to identify once you know for what you are looking. There exist signals that alert us to the Latinate influence:

- Latinate words contain a root with a prefix and/or a suffix, as in "com" + "plic" + "ate."

- Latinate words contain "-ct" or "-pt" as final blends, as in "instinct," "wept," and "duct."

- Latinate words have double consonants as a result of assimilated prefixes, as in "connect," illusion," and "accept."

- Latinate words contain "-ti-," "-si-," and "-ci-" that say / *sh* /, as in "partition," "musician," and "mission."

An in-depth listing of the Latinate roots, their meanings, and examples can be found in Appendix C. Another in-depth listing, with the Latinate prefixes, their meanings, and examples, can be found in Appendix D.

Assimilated Latinate prefixes. Assimilated prefixes, also known as "chameleon" prefixes, are Latinate prefixes that change based upon the Latinate roots that are attached to them. The definition of the prefix does not change; however, the spelling does. There are seven assimilated or "chameleon" prefixes: "ad-," "con-," "dis-," "ex-," "in-," "ob-," and "sub-." Many believe that six of these may be introduced in pairs to students because they make similar changes: "con-" and "in-," "dis-" and "ex-," and "ob-" and "sub-." I have discovered that this serves to confuse more than enlighten, because the changes are not identical. I would suggest that each individual assimilated prefix be introduced separately and in its entirety. A full list of various words that can be used to teach the assimilated Latinate prefixes to students can be found at http://www.prufrock.com/assets/clientpages/schoolsuccessdyslexia. aspx.

The prefix "ad-" makes nine changes based upon the root to which it is attached.:

- "ad-" becomes "ac-" before a "c" or a "q," as in "accomplish" or "acquit";
- "ad-" becomes "af-" before an "f, " as in "affect";
- "ad-" becomes "ag-" before a "g," as in "aggressive";
- "ad-" becomes "al-" before an "l," as in "allude";
- "ad-" becomes "an-" before an "n," as in "annex";
- "ad-" becomes "ap-" before a "p," as in "appear";
- "ad-" becomes "ar-" before an "r," as in "arrogant";
- "ad-" becomes "as-" before an "s" or a soft "c," as in "assumption" and "ascent"; and
- "ad-" becomes "at-" before a "t," as in "attraction."

The prefix "con-" makes four changes based upon the root to which it is attached:

- "con-" becomes "col-" before an "l," as in "collegiate";
- "con-" becomes "com-" before an "m," "p," or "b," as in "committee," "compel," and "combat";
- "con-" becomes "cor-" before an "r," as in "corrupt"; and

- "con-" becomes "co-" before an "h" or a vowel, as in "cohabit" and "coauthor."

The prefix "dis-" makes two changes based upon the root to which it is attached:

- "dis-" becomes "dif-" before an "f, " as in "different" and "difficulty"; and
- "dis-" becomes "di-" before an "m," "v," "l," or "g," as in "dimension," "diverge," "dilute," and "digest."

The prefix "ex-" makes two changes based upon the root to which it is attached:

- "ex-" becomes "ef-" before an "f," as in "effort" and "effigy"; and
- "ex-" becomes "e-" before a "d," "l," "m," "n," or "v," as in "education," "elevate," "emergency," "enunciate," and "evade."

The prefix "in-" makes three changes based upon the root to which it is attached:

- "in-" becomes "il-" before an "l," as in "illustrate";
- "in-" becomes "im-" before an "m," "p," or "b," as in "immune," "impolite," and "imburse"; and
- "in-" becomes "ir-" before an "r," as in "irregular."

The prefix "ob-" makes three changes based upon the root to which it is attached:

- "ob-" becomes "oc-" before a "c," as in "occupy";
- "ob-" becomes "of-" before an "f," as in "offend"; and
- "ob-" becomes "op-" before a "p," as in "opponent."

The prefix "sub-" makes six changes based upon the root to which it is attached.

- "sub-" becomes "suc-" before a "c," as in "success";
- "sub-" becomes "suf-" before an "f," as in "sufficient";
- "sub-" becomes "sug-" before a "g," as in "suggestion";
- "sub-" becomes "sup-" before a "p," as in "supportive";
- "sub-" becomes "sur-" before an "r," "as in "surreal"; and
- "sub-" becomes "sus-" before a "t," as in "sustain."

Latinate Connectives

In Latinate word construction, the vowels "u," "o," and "i" are used to connect a root to a suffix. In this context, the three vowels function as connectives. There are three Latinate connectives with which we are concerned: "i," "u," and "ul."[16]

The Latinate connective "i" is the most commonly used of the three Latinate connectives. The connective "i" represents two different sounds:

- When it is followed by a vowel suffix, the Latinate connective "i " says / ē /, as in "feet" as in the following words: "lenient," "mania," "aviary," "radio," and "exterior."

- When it appears after an "l" or an "n," the Latinate connective "i " maintains the sound / ē / but the letter that follows the Latinate connective "i " is reduced to a schwa, / ə /, which is pronounced like the "u" in "hut." The Latinate connective "i " flows right into the following reduced vowel. It sounds like / ē / / ə /. You can easily hear the sound / ē / / ə / in words like "million" (/ m / / ĭ / / l / / ē / / ə / / n /). Notice the application and the location of the Latinate connective "i " and the reduced vowel that follows as the two say / ē / / ə / in the following words: "stallion," "valiant," "onion," "insignia," and "spaniel."

---

16 There is a fourth Latinate connective, "ol." However, it occurs so rarely that I do not teach it.

The Latinate connectives "u" and "ul" are always pronounced with a long "u" phoneme, as found in the word "few." Notice the application of the Latinate connectives "u" and "ul" as the "u" says / $\bar{u}$ / in the following words: "manual," "evacuate," "particular," and "peculiar."

The "-du-" (/ j / / $\bar{u}$ /) and the "-tu-" (/ ch / / $\bar{u}$ /) are created when the letters "d" or "t" appear in front of the Latinate connectives "u" and "ul."

- When a "d" appears in front of "u," it says / j / / $\bar{u}$ /, as in "graduate," "residual," "deciduous," individual," and "education."

- When a "d" appears in front of "ul," it says / j / / $\bar{u}$ / / l /, as in "modular," "schedule," and "nodule."

- When a "t" appears in front of "u," it says / ch / / $\bar{u}$ /, as in "fortune," "spiritual," "infatuate," "natural," "century," and "actual."

- When a "t" appears in front of "ul," it says / ch / / $\bar{u}$ / / l /, as in "postulate," "congratulate," "spatula," and "tarantula."

A full list of various words that can be used to teach the Latinate connectives to students can be found at http://www.prufrock.com/assets/clientpages/schoolsuccessdyslexia.aspx.

Anglo-Saxon Word Construction

Anglo-Saxon word construction lays the foundation for reading skills in the English code. Students will first encounter Anglo-Saxon word construction at the very beginning of their formal education, and this will extend throughout the rest of their lives. Please remember that practically 100% of the words that students will encounter from prekindergarten through the third grade are based upon Anglo-Saxon word construction.

Anglo-Saxon word construction is where we get our sight words. Sight words are words that are nonphonetic, meaning they are not spelled the way that they sound. Chapter 3 included information on teaching children to learn sight words. We also encounter silent letters, consonant digraphs, consonant blends, and vowel teams in Anglo-Saxon word construction (see Chapter 4 for more information on each of these areas).

Anglo-Saxon word construction is where we get our spelling rules:

- the cvc doubling rule;
- the long spelling rule for "-ck";
- the long spelling rule for "-dge";
- the long spelling rule for "-tch";
- the "f," "l," "s" doubling rule;
- the "y" rule; and
- the silent "e" rule.

Each of these rules is explained in detail in Chapter 4, pages 104–109.

These are five components that may play a role in the construction of an Anglo-Saxon word.

- **Base word:** A base word is a word of Anglo-Saxon origin that can stand alone and still have meaning, such as "house," "board," "fish," and "cat."

- **Compound word:** A compound word is a word composed of two base words. Together, the words are given a new meaning, such as "handbag" and "houseboat."

- **Prefix:** A prefix is a letter or phonogram that is added to beginning of a base word. The addition of a prefix changes the meaning of the base word, such as the word "understand," with the prefix being "under."

- **Suffix:** A suffix is a letter or phonogram that is added to the end of a base word. The addition of a suffix changes the meaning of the base word, such as the word "neighborhood," with the suffix being "hood."

- **Derivatives:** A derivative is a base word plus a suffix, such as the words "working" and "seated." The suffixes here are "ing" and "ed."

Anglo-Saxon word construction may appear in five different forms:

- **Base word:** These are words such as "ship," "flow," "house," and "knife."

- **Base word + base word (a.k.a., a compound word):** Take the Anglo-Saxon base word "cat" and another Anglo-Saxon base word "fish," combine them, and you get the compound word "catfish."

- **Prefix + base word:** Take the Anglo-Saxon prefix "mid-" and the Anglo-Saxon base word "night," combine them, and you get the word "midnight."

- **Base word + suffix:** Take the Anglo-Saxon base word "get" and the Anglo-Saxon suffix "-ing," combine them, and you get the word "getting."

- **Prefix + base word + suffix:** Take the Anglo-Saxon prefix "over-," the Anglo-Saxon base word "sleep," and the Anglo-Saxon suffix "-ing," combine them, and you get the word "oversleeping."

Identifying Words of Anglo-Saxon Origin

Words of Anglo-Saxon origin, like those of Latinate and Greek origins, are easy to identify once you know for what you are looking. Like the Latinate, Greek, and French codes, there are signals that alert us to the Anglo-Saxon influence:

- Anglo-Saxon words have silent letters that at one time during the evolution of the language were pronounced. However, today the letters are silent, as in the words "know," ghost," "tomb," and "write."

- Anglo-Saxon words have consonant digraphs (see Chapter 4), as in "bath," "thing," "ship," and "lunch."

- Anglo-Saxon words have k's, as in "king," "bike," "kiss," and "kill."

- Anglo-Saxon words have w's, as in "with," "wind," "jaw," and "well."

- Anglo-Saxon words have vowel digraphs (see Chapter 4),[17] as in "coat," "leak," "teen," and "new."

- Anglo-Saxon words have double consonants, as in "kettle," "rabbit," "mitten," and "killer."

- Anglo-Saxon words have consonant blends (see Chapter 4), as in "whisper," "stolen," "splash," and "sister."

Greek Word Construction

Familiarizing your students with Greek word construction will prove invaluable with respect to advanced vocabulary. Although only 11% of the words in the English code are Greek in origin, the overwhelming majority of words used in science, math, and medicine are Greek in origin or are a combination of Greek and Latin.

There are two main components that may play a role in the construction of a Greek word. Similar to Anglo-Saxon compound words, most Greek words are made of two parts called *combining forms*. The combining forms have been labeled by many as prefixes, roots, connectives, and suffixes. In order to simplify this presentation, we will view

17 Though it does occur, it is uncommon for Latinate or Greek word construction to contain vowel teams.

the parts that play a role in Greek word construction by three names: combining forms, the connective, and the suffix.

- **Combining forms:** The combining form functions as an Anglo-Saxon base word does in that the combining form is a word part to which other combining forms are added in order to create words. However, whereas Anglo-Saxon base words need not have a suffix or a prefix in order to exist as a whole, the Greek combining forms must be attached to at least one other Greek combining form to exist as a whole word. For example, take a look at the word "telephone." The word "telephone" is composed of two Greek combining forms: the first, "tele," and the second, "phon." The second combining form, "phon," means "sound." The first, "tele," means "distant" or "far." So, "telephone" means "distant (or far) sound."

- **Connective:** The Greek connective is the letter "o." It is not always necessary to use a connective in the creation of a Greek word. In the previous example, the first combining form, "tele," was added to the second combining form, "phon," to create the word "telephone." No connective was needed. However, in many situations, the connective "o" is required. For example, take the word "photograph." The word "photograph" is composed of two combining forms: the first, "phot," and the second, "graph." However, "photgraph" is not a correct word. It becomes correct, however, when we place a connective "o" in between the two combining forms to unite them: "phot" + "o" + "graph"= "photograph."

- **Suffix:** A suffix is a letter or phonogram that is added to the end of a combining form. The addition of a suffix changes the tense or part of speech of the combining form. Most Greek words do not have suffixes unless we are applying a scientific view upon the word. In those cases, it will usually refer to the quality of a person or a thing. Even under these circumstances, the suffix will most likely be of Latinate origin. For example, take the word "hieroglyphic," which is composed of two combining forms joined by the connective "o": "hier" and "glyph."

Yet, "hier" + "o" + "glyph" is combined with a Latinate suffix, "-ic," to create the scientifically referenced term "hieroglyphic."

Greek construction may appear in a variety of different forms. Because Greek word construction rules allow us to use more than one connective "o" and multiple combining forms, we shall discuss only two basic constructive formats:

- combining form + combining form = word, and

- combining form + connective + combining form = word.

Let's provide an example of each of these.

- As an example of combining form + combining form = word, we have the Greek combining form "poly," which means "many." We have the Greek combining form "gon," which means "angle." We combine them, and we get the word "polygon." A polygon is a shape with many angles.

- As an example of combining form + connective + combining form = word, we have the Greek combining form "therm," which means "heat." We have our connective "o." Lastly, we have the Greek combining form "meter," which means "measure." We combine them, and we get the word "thermometer." A thermometer measures heat.

The Greek Code

The Greek code serves as an indication that the student is dealing with a word of Greek origin. There are three components that indicate a word of Greek origin: "ch," "ph," and "y."

- When the "ch" says / k /, as in "chrome" (/ k / / r / / $\bar{o}$ / / m /), the word is of Greek origin. Notice the application of "ch" as it says / k / in the following words: "orchestra," "anchor," "charisma," "monarch," "chasm," "synchronize," and "echo."

- When the "ph" says / f /, as in "phone" (/ f / / ō / / n /), the word is of Greek origin. Notice the application of "ph" as it says / f / in the following words: "elephant," "philosophy," "cipher," "phenomenon," "atmosphere," "trophy," "phobia," and "gopher."

- When the "y" says / ĭ /, as in "hit" (/ h / / ĭ / / t /) or / ī /, as in "bike" (/ b / / ī / / k /), the word is of Greek origin. Notice the application of "y" as it says / ĭ / or / ī / in the following words: "gym," "cyclone," "type," "cryptic," "mystery," "symbol," "python," and "hyphen."

A full list of various words that can be used to teach the Greek code to students can be found at http://www.prufrock.com/assets/clientpages/schoolsuccessdyslexia.aspx.

Identifying Words of Greek Origin

Words of Greek origin, like those of Anglo-Saxon and Latinate origin, are easy to identify once you know for what you are looking. Like the Latinate code and the French code, signals exist that alert us to the Greek influence:

- Greek words contain a "ph" that says / f /, as in "typhoon," "telephone," and "phobia."

- Greek words contain a "ch" that says / k /, as in "chrome," "Christmas," and "charisma."

- Greek words contain a "y" that says / ĭ / or / ī /, as in "bicycle," "myth," and "style."

- Greek words use a silent "p," as in "psychology" and "pneumonia."

- Greek words use a silent "m," as in "mnemonic."

Appendix E contains a list of the various Greek combining forms, their meanings, and examples.

Assimilated Greek Prefix

There is one Greek combining form that operates similar to the assimilated Latinate prefixes (see pp. 123–126): "syn-." It, too, changes based upon the Greek combining form that it is attached to. Again, the definition of the prefix does not change; however, the spelling does.

The Greek combining form "syn-" makes three changes based upon the Greek combining form to which it is attached:

- "syn-" becomes "syl-" before an "l," as in "syllable";
- "syn-" becomes "sym-" before an "m," "p," or "b," as in "symmetry," "symphony," and "symbol"; and
- "syn-" becomes "sys-" before a "t," as in "system."

A full list of various words that can be used to teach the assimilated Greek prefix to students can be found at http://www.prufrock.com/assets/clientpages/schoolsuccessdyslexia.aspx.

The French Code

The French code serves as an indication that the student is dealing with a word of French origin. Although less than 3% of words found in the English code are derived from the French code, 3% of the estimated 1.2 million words in the English code is quite a substantial number. There are four components that indicate a word of French origin: "que," "qu," "ch," and "i":

- When the "que" says / k /, as in "king," the word is of French origin. Notice the application and the location of "que" as it says / *k* / in the following words: "plaque," "unique," "baroque," "opaque," "antique," and "critique."

- When the "qu" says / *k* /, as in "king," the word is of French origin. Notice the application and the location of "qu" as it says / *k* / in the following words: "mosquito," "turquoise," lacquer," "mannequin," "conquer," "etiquette," and "bouquet."

- When "ch" says / *sh* /, as in "ship," the word is of French origin. Notice the application and the location of "ch" as it says / *sh* / in the following words: "chauvinist," "chaise," "brochure," "gauche," "parachute," and "chef."

- When "i" says / *ē* / as in "feet," the word is of French origin. Notice the application and the location of "i " as it says / *ē* / in the following words: "machine," "fiancée," "chic," "praline," "elite," "sardine," "routine," and "unique."

In the French code, the "q" functions similarly to how it functions in the English code in that the "q" never appears without a "u" immediately following it. However, that is where the similarities end. In the French code, the "q" and the "u" function as a consonant digraph as they work together to say / *k* /.

A full list of various words that can be used to teach the French code to students can be found at http://www.prufrock.com/assets/clientpages/schoolsuccessdyslexia.aspx.

Chapter Summary

Mastering the English code is clearly a huge task. A systematic and explicit approach to morphology will assist students and provide a crucial foundation for the development of vocabulary, enhancing a student's comprehension and decoding skills. Now that we have our general framework within which to work, let's provide a more structured approach to language remediation in Chapter 6.

A More Specific Strategy for Remediation:

A Structured Plan for Teachers and Parents

A S I prepared to write this book, I asked many of my clients what they would like to see included. An overwhelming response was, "I wish someone would show me how to do it myself. I want to help my child, but I don't know how much longer I will be able to afford you." This comment was rather timely, given the economic climate. Academic language therapy sessions can cost $90–$125 per hour. If you have the suggested minimum numbers of sessions per week (two), parents are spending $720–$1,000 per month to provide support from a qualified language-training instructor. Keep in mind that we are not discussing normal tutoring. Most students who have learning disabilities do not respond to normal tutoring. This is due to the fact that these students have visual processing deficits, auditory processing deficits, or both. Normal tutoring attempts to address academic issues using either visual or auditory processing, when a multisensory approach is required in order to overcome deficits in academic language.

Academic Language

Academic language represents the complex components of the English language that are required for success in academic discourse. In vocabulary and structure, it is quite different from the social English that we use in normal conversations. Mainly composed of Latinate and Greek word construction, academic language is the primary hindrance to the comprehension of school texts and lectures. Therefore, poor academic language skills are the root of low academic performance.

To combat poor academic language skills, students will require instruction in the following key areas of academic language development:

- **vocabulary:** knowledge of the forms and meanings of words;

- **grammar:** knowledge of the grammatical rules that govern usage;

- **sentence structure:** using words to convey simple and complex thoughts;

- **Latinate word construction:** knowledge of prefixes, roots, connectives, suffixes;

- **Greek word construction:** knowledge of combining forms (roots) and the connective "o";

- **sociolinguistics:** the ability to vary language appropriately;

- **critical thinking skills:** the ability to analyze, compare, contrast, and other skills;

- **language awareness:** knowledge of academic writing structure;

- **study skills:** knowledge of how to review, test preparation, and other strategies; and

- **learning styles:** knowledge of what methods allow us to maximize our educational experience.

Although this book is not intended to supplant the highly qualified academic language therapist, I do hope to provide parents with some relief by giving them tools and strategies that may be done at home to aid in remediation during these financially trying times.

Academic Language Therapy

Academic language therapy helps students who need primary instruction or remediation with the English code. Because the educational experience of American students is conducted primarily in the English language, adequate language skills are essential for school success. Academic language therapy, therefore, serves as a foundation for lifelong learning.

Utilizing the multisensory strategies that are the cornerstone of the Orton-Gillingham approach, academic language therapy is designed to meet the needs of students who are struggling with reading, writing, and spelling due to auditory and visual processing deficits or language-based learning disorders such as dyslexia.

Typically, academic language therapy services may include, but are not limited to:

- phonology,

- decoding (word attack skills),

- morphology,

- handwriting,

- composition,

- reading fluency and comprehension,
- writing mechanics,
- spelling,
- learning strategies,
- study skills,
- exam preparation, and
- SAT/ACT preparation.

In order to provide teachers and parents with a multisensory approach that would meet their encoding and decoding needs, I had to narrow my focus and deal only with the issues that relate to the foundation of reading and spelling (phonology, decoding, morphology, and encoding). Although the remaining areas are of great importance for students who are struggling with the language acquisition process, they could not be addressed sufficiently within this work.

Scope and Sequence

As we begin down the road to remediation, we must remember that students will need specific things depending upon their stage of development. More clearly stated, students in kindergarten through the end of third grade will not need the Latinate word construction study that those in grades 4–7 will need, because students do not encounter Latinate word construction until approximately the fourth grade. Additionally, those in grades 7 and beyond will need to learn Anglo-Saxon word construction and Latinate word construction prior to commencing the study of Greek word construction and vocabulary development.

Later in this chapter, I share a plan for creating remediation lessons. In addition to the daily phonemic awareness drills and phonics deck review included in these lessons, I recommend the following scope and sequence as teachers and parents pursue English code remediation:

- Phonemic Awareness Drills [Each class session should begin with phonemic awareness drills and the phonics deck.]
  - phoneme replication
  - phoneme segmentation
  - phoneme blending
  - phoneme substitution
  - rhyming

- Phonics Deck Review
- Word Attack Skills
  - short vowels
  - long vowels
  - consonants
  - consonant digraphs
  - consonant blends
  - vowel glides

- Phonology
  - syllable types
    - open
    - closed

  - silent "e" syllables
  - vowel digraphs
  - "r"-controlled syllables
  - consonant + "le" syllables
  - final stable syllables

- Syllable Division
  - vc/cv
  - v/cv
  - vc/v

- Spelling
  - long vowel spellings
  - rare long vowel spellings
  - vowel teams
  - the two sounds of "oo"
  - the two sounds of "ou"
  - the two sounds of "ow"
  - the two sounds of "c"
  - the two sounds of "g"
  - the two sounds of "s"
  - the three sounds of "-ed"
  - the three sounds of "ea"
  - the three sounds of "y"
  - "au" versus "aw"
  - "ie" and "ei"
  - "oi" versus "oy"
  - "ou" versus "ow"
  - the long spelling rule
  - the "f," "l," "s" doubling rule
  - the cvc doubling rule
  - the silent "e" rule
  - the "y" rule

- Morphology
  - ○ Anglo-Saxon word construction
  - ○ identifying words of Anglo-Saxon origin
  - ○ Latinate word construction
  - ○ identifying words of Latinate origin
  - ○ Latinate roots and prefixes
  - ○ Greek word construction
  - ○ identifying words of Greek construction

This list may look daunting, but remember that all of these items have been discussed in detail with examples in Chapters 3, 4, and 5. Parents and teachers can flip to these previous chapters to review each of the concepts listed. Also remember that the Orton-Gillingham approach is diagnostic-prescriptive. At any given moment, you may need to review a previously mastered concept in order to properly present a new concept.

The Student Notebook

Each student who undergoes remediation must have a student notebook or student manual that is properly maintained. The purpose of the proper maintenance of a student notebook is to provide the student with a fully functioning resource guide. It is imperative that the student notebook remain current and that the material be legibly written in ink using uniform, cursive writing. The cursive writing serves as a reinforcement of the cursive writing required of all Orton-Gillingham students, and the ink adds durability to the information. This notebook should be carried at all times that homework is attempted or a language training session is in progress.

The student notebook should be presented as a blank edition of a phonics resource guide. You may use any type of notebook that you wish, although I have found that the marble composition books available from dollar stores will work just fine. The pages should be numbered throughout the composition book, and this guide should be filled in by the teacher/parent at the time new material is presented. Teachers and parents are encouraged to cover only the material that the student needs to learn and to place the information within the resource guide.

Writing in the Student Notebook

There are several basic sources of information that should be placed in the student notebook immediately:

1. **The lower- and uppercase cursive alphabet:** The alphabet should be written on the first few pages of the student notebook in black ink. The letters should be neatly formed and written separately, and proper spacing should be applied between each cursive letter. The lowercase alphabet should be written first, with "a–m" on one line and "n–z" written two lines below. Four lines should be skipped before writing the uppercase alphabet in the same fashion. At the bottom of the page, the parent should leave nine lines upon which to print the lower- and uppercase alphabets as a resource for the student.

2. **Short vowels:** The short vowels should be placed on a separate page. The label at the top of the page should clearly read "Short Vowels." Next to each vowel, the parent should include a key word that the student can use to remember the short vowel sound, like "stop" for the short "o" or "bed" for the short "e." If the student is young enough or so inclined, space may be left for the student to illustrate key words (or the parent may take on this endeavor). Next to the key word, the letter should be written between two right-slanted lines with the diacritical

mark applied. This will indicate to the student the sound that the grapheme makes (e.g., / ŏ /).

3. **Long vowels:** The long vowels should be placed on a separate page. The label at the top of the page should clearly read "Long Vowels." Next to each vowel, the parent should include a key word that the student can use to remember the long vowel sound, like "boat" for the long "o" or "teeth" for the long "e." Again, space may be left for the student to illustrate key words (or the parent may take on this endeavor). Next to the key word, the letter should be written between two right-slanted lines with the diacritical mark applied (e.g., / ē /).

4. **Consonants:** The consonants should be placed on a separate page. The label at the top of the page should clearly read "Consonants." Next to each consonant, the parent should include a key word that the student can use to remember the consonant sound, like "bat" for "b" or "nose" for "n." Again, space may be left for the student to illustrate key words (or the parent may take on this endeavor.) Next to the key word, the letter should be written between two right-slanted lines (e.g., / n /).

The four items mentioned above will provide a wonderful beginning to the student notebook. From this point forward, each new concept introduced to the student must be written in the student notebook. This will serve as a visual resource for the student as well as a time saver for the parent when the time arises to review or reinforce a concept.

The Assessments

The assessments are the first step in the creation of your home therapy operation, and I recommend that you use three: the Assessment of Sound/Symbol Correspondence (ASSC), the Diagnostic Deck, and the Spelling Deck Administration Form. The Assessment of

Sound/Symbol Correspondence administration form (p. 221) and the Spelling Deck Administration Form (p. 233) are found in Appendices F and G. The Diagnostic Deck will be created by the parent/teacher following the instructions below. Clearly you need to assess where your child is in order to properly serve her needs. You have already read her scores and reports from various diagnostic tests the school has conducted, and you know that your child has a difficult time reading. Now, let's find out what she knows about the English code. For example, does she know what sound "eigh" makes when she sees it? Do she know that "a," "a-e," "ai," "ay," "ea," "ei," "eigh," and "ey" all say / $\bar{a}$ /, as in "way," "whey," or "weigh"? Let's determine this. We will begin with the Diagnostic Deck that you are going to make.

The Diagnostic Deck

The Diagnostic Deck shall be comprised of 63 cards. The words on these cards (see pages 147–153) have been specifically chosen for the phonemes, graphemes, phonograms, syllabication, and spelling rules involved in both the spelling and reading of the words. Print one word on each card. Through the use of this deck, the parent will be given a clear picture of what the student understands and can apply, and equally, what the student must experience in order to be a successful reader and speller.

The cards should be unnumbered and one sided, and you may proceed in the order you deem necessary. However, documentation on the Diagnostic Deck Assessment Form (found in Appendix H) of what is mispronounced or misspelled must be accurate in order to properly serve the student.

The creation of the Diagnostic Deck is designed with two end products in mind: the classroom set (8.5" by 11") and the individual set (3" by 5") to be used when involved in one-on-one or small-group remediation. Obviously, the classroom set is placed on larger paper with bigger print so that the words may be seen more readily. Merely place one of the words (see the following list) in large print in the center of each card. I recommend that you use a black marker and basic print as you create your drill cards. The black print on the white background will create a contrast that will aid in visual tracking. Lastly, I recommend that you print the cards on cardstock (for the class set) and index cards (for the individual set). Either may be purchased at any office supply store. This will ensure that the cards will be a part of your class or home therapy operation for quite some time. Once you have your Diagnostic Deck created, place a rubber band around it to keep it together. Then, place it in a box large enough to store them with your drill cards (see p. 156) so that you may find them quickly.

Below is an examination of each card's word in the Diagnostic Deck and the language skills that are associated, on all levels, with the word on the card. Remember, the cards in the Diagnostic Deck should just have the word listed in bold on the card—the additional skills listed are for you to understand the concepts associated with the mastery of the word. They let you understand that if the child is able to read the word, he may have an understanding of the concepts listed. If the child is not able to read the word, you now know that the child is having difficulties with the concepts associated with the word. For example, if the child cannot read the word "ceiling," perhaps the child struggles with the two sounds of "c" or the vowel team "ei."

ceiling
soft "c"
"ie"/ "ei" spellings
long vowel spellings
"-ing" suffix
closed syllables
vowel team syllables

belief
open syllables
"ie"/ "ei" spellings
long vowel spellings
tiger syllable division
vowel team syllables

sneaker
initial blends
three sounds of "ea"
vowel-"r" that says / ər /
"r"-controlled syllables
vowel team syllables

market
vowel-"r" that says / ar /
"r"-controlled syllables
short vowels
closed syllables
rabbit syllable division

confuse
long vowel spellings
rabbit syllable division
Latinate prefix "con-"
two sounds of "s"
closed syllables
the schwa

misjudge
long spelling rule
closed syllables
rabbit syllable division

applaud
Latinate prefix "ad-"
closed syllables
sound of "au"
initial blends
vowel team syllables

stable
open syllables
initial blends
consonant + "le" syllables
tiger syllable division

squeamish
two sounds of "s"
three sounds of "ea"
digraphs
English code "qu"
closed syllables
vowel team syllables

handshake
closed syllables
final blends
digraphs
long vowel spellings
silent "e" syllables

patched
long spelling rule
closed syllables
three sounds of "-ed"

postpone
closed syllables
final blends
long vowel spellings
"-ost" spelling
silent "e" syllables

scissors
silent "c"
two sounds of "s"
vowel-"r" that says / ər /
closed syllables
"r"-controlled syllables

pony
long vowel spellings
final "y"
tiger syllable division
open syllables

lucky
closed syllables
long spelling rule
final "y"

gargle
vowel-"r" that says / *ar* /
consonant + "le" syllables
two sounds of "g"
"r"-controlled syllables

necktie
closed syllables
long spelling rule
rare long vowel spellings

feudal
rare long vowel spellings
"-al" suffix
vowel team syllables
the schwa

immerse
Latinate prefix "in-"
vowel-"r" that says / *ər* /
two sounds of "s"
"r"-controlled syllables
rabbit syllable division

extreme
Latinate prefix "ex-"
long vowel spelling
initial blends
silent "e" syllables

juice
soft "c"
rare long vowel spellings
vowel team syllables

chorus
Greek code "ch"
vowel-"r" that says / *or* /
"-us" suffix
"r"-controlled syllables

thirsty
digraphs
vowel-"r" that says / *ər* /
final blends
final "y"
"r"-controlled syllables

daybreak
vowel spellings
initial blends
long spelling rule
three sounds of "ea"
vowel team syllables

spider
initial blends
long vowel spellings
vowel-"r" that says / ər /
"r"-controlled syllables
tiger syllable division

eighteen
long vowel spellings
vowel team syllables
rare long vowel spellings

reindeer
long vowel spellings
rabbit syllable division
vowel team syllables
rare long vowel spelling

whistle
digraphs
silent "t"
consonant + "le" syllables
closed syllables
the schwa

quality
English code "qu"
final "y"
closed syllables

pillow
closed syllables
long vowel spellings
rabbit syllable division
"f," "l," "s" doubling rule
vowel team syllables

freedom
initial blends
long vowel spellings
the schwa
tiger syllable division

symbol
Greek code "y"
rabbit syllable division
the schwa

baby
long vowel spellings
tiger syllable division
final "y"
open syllables

sniffle
closed syllables
initial blends
consonant + "le" syllables
the schwa

ointment
"oi" versus "oy"
diphthongs
final blends
"-ment" suffix

freestyle
initial blends
long vowel spellings
Greek code "y"
vowel team syllables

dismay
Latinate prefix "dis-"
long vowel spellings
rabbit syllable division
closed syllables
open syllables
vowel team syllables

sewer
long vowel spellings
vowel-"r" that says / ər /
"r"-controlled syllables
vowel team syllables

spongy
closed syllables
two sounds of "g"
final "y"
rabbit syllable division
initial blends
open syllables

bouncing
"ou" versus "ow"
diphthongs
two sounds of "c"
"-ing" suffix
silent "e" rule

argue
vowel-"r" that says / ar /
two sounds of "g"
long vowel spellings
rabbit syllable division
open syllables
vowel team syllables

complain
Latinate prefix "con-"
initial blends
long vowel spellings
closed syllables
vowel team syllables
the schwa

midnight
closed syllables
long vowel spellings
rabbit syllable division

allow
Latinate prefix "ad-"
"ou" versus "ow"
diphthongs
the schwa

youthful
consonant digraphs
"-ful" suffix
two sounds of "ou"
the schwa
closed syllables
vowel team syllables

threaten
initial blends
three sounds of "ea"
"-en" suffix
closed syllables
vowel team syllables

bemoan
open syllables
long vowel spellings
tiger syllable division
vowel team syllables

survey
vowel-"r" that says / ər /
rabbit syllable division
long vowel spellings
vowel team syllables
"r"-controlled syllables

typhoon
long vowel spellings
Greek code "y"
open syllables
tiger syllable division
vowel team syllables

music
open syllables
long vowel spellings
two sounds of "c"
closed syllables
two sounds of "s"
tiger syllable division

valley
long vowel spellings
closed syllables
rabbit syllable division
"f," "l," "s" doubling rule
vowel team syllables

backhoe
long spelling rule
rare long vowel spellings
closed syllables
vowel team syllables

recite
open syllables
long vowel spellings
two sounds of "c"
Latinate prefix "re-"
silent "e" syllables

distort
Latinate prefix "dis-"
vowel-"r" that says / or /
"r"-controlled syllables
initial blends
rabbit syllable division

rolled
three sounds of "-ed"
"-oll" spellings

childhood
"-ild" spellings
consonant digraphs
vowel team syllables
two sounds of "oo"

bluffing
initial blends
"f," "l," "s" doubling rule
"-ing" suffix
closed syllables

secret
open syllables
long vowel spellings
two sounds of "c"
closed syllables
two sounds of "s"
tiger syllable division

mushroom
consonant digraphs
two sounds of "oo"
vowel team syllables
closed syllables

curfew
vowel-"r" that says / ər /
long vowel spellings
"r"-controlled syllables
two sounds of "c"
rabbit syllable division
vowel team syllables

mustache
French code "ch"
closed syllables
final blends

beggar
vowel-"r" that says / ər /
two sounds of "g"
closed syllables
"r"-controlled syllables

dawdle
consonant + "le
vowel team syllables
"au" versus "aw"

The Diagnostic Procedure

Ideally, the initial diagnostic process should be done over 2 days. The Assessment of Sound/Symbol Correspondence (ASSC) and the reading diagnostic test (using the Diagnostic Deck) should be administered first. Although the ASSC is the foundational assessment by which you will remediate your child's language difficulties, the Diagnostic Deck will play a crucial role as well. That is why I am suggesting that you use both. Even if your child does not correctly identify a phoneme on the ASSC, yet is able to read a word on a card on day 1 with said phoneme *and* spell a word on the card with said phoneme on day 2, it is a fair assessment that the material represented by the word need not be covered initially. There is most likely a more pressing issue or concept that should be addressed. Your child may have developed compensatory strategies (e.g., a strong sight word vocabulary) that will continue to serve him for a short period of time while you address more problematic issues. Slowly, the parent will be able to identify the most glaring deficits and address them accordingly. A weekly review of the Diagnostic Deck cards as either a reading or spelling deck will serve to keep the parent abreast of any problems that may surface or of material that has not been retained by the student.

Day 1. On the first day, the teacher or parent will use the Recording Form of the Assessment of Sound/Symbol Correspondence (see pp. 222–225). The student should be given the Reading Form of the ASSC (see pp. 226–231) and an index card with which to keep his place. Then, moving vertically throughout the entire assessment, the student will give the sound(s) represented by each phoneme. If the student does not know the sound(s) represented by the phoneme, he should say, "I don't know." Remind him that there is no shame in this. Place a check next to the phoneme and the sound(s) that it represents. Likewise, if the student provides an incorrect sound for a phoneme, place a check next to the phoneme and the sound(s) that it represents. This is the manner for proceeding throughout each section of the Reading Form. Once the student has completed the Reading Form, the parent should tally the check marks and record the information on the Recording Form. If the student properly identifies the sound(s) represented by the phoneme, leave the blank empty. If, however, the student encounters a phoneme that makes multiple sounds (like "ch" that says / *ch* /, / *k* /, and / *sh* /), and he pauses after giving one sound, the parent may prompt the student by saying, "and."

After the ASSC has been completed, take the newly created Diagnostic Deck in hand and have the student read the word on the face of the card aloud. Each card that is read appropriately should be placed on the table directly in front of you. If a student hesitates, stammers, or mispronounces a word, it constitutes inappropriate identification. Cards that are inappropriately identified should be placed to the right of you. The deck that remains on the right should be properly documented on the Diagnostic Deck Assessment Form. The phonograms, spelling patterns, and spelling rules should be coordinated with the results of the Assessment of Sound/Symbol Correspondence. Together, this record will serve as a clear starting point from which you may begin as you follow the lesson plans outlined later in this chapter.

Day 2. On the second day, the procedure is somewhat different. Instead of allowing the student to read the word, you should read the word to the student using the Spelling Deck Administration Form. Following the protocol for the administration of the spelling diagnostic, say the word, use the word in the sentence supplied on the Spelling Deck Administration Form, and repeat the word. After you say the word the second time, the student must write its correct spelling on a separate sheet of paper. I discourage you from repeating the word beyond the recommended procedure. If the student is unable to clearly understand the words you pronounce, this information must be clearly documented. If this occurs frequently during the diagnostic, it is possible that the student may have a central auditory processing deficit. Further testing by a qualified speech and language pathologist may be necessary. Words on the Spelling Deck Administration Form that are spelled incorrectly should be documented and coordinated with the Diagnostic Deck and the Assessment of Sound/Symbol Correspondence and used as a starting point for providing the necessary remediation of spelling rules and generalizations.

On the spelling test, students who are capable of writing in cursive should be encouraged to do so. Students who are incapable of writing in cursive or who demonstrate a labored presentation in letter formation should be allowed to write in print.

After the assessments are completed, parents and teachers have a clear picture of the student's strengths and weaknesses. Moving from the simple to the more complex, parents and teachers may proceed according to the scope and sequence of the structured approach in this chapter. Start with the most glaring weakness and move forward. Remember, skills that build upon other skills are placed accordingly in the proper place within the scope and sequence.

How to Create the Drill Cards

The drill cards serve a vital function toward the success of the Orton-Gillingham approach. Remember that the Orton-Gillingham approach revolves around the scientifically based concepts that humans acquire and master language through three distinct neurological pathways: visual processing (seeing), auditory processing (hearing), and tactile-kinesthetic processing (feeling). Therefore, after a concept has been formally introduced (by direct instruction), it must be drilled if the student is to remember the information. Drilling will be classified under two simple headings: decoding (reading) and encoding (spelling).

The creation of the drill cards is designed with two end products in mind: the classroom set (8.5" by 11") and the individual set (3" by 5") to be used when involved in one-to-one or small-group remediation. Obviously, the classroom set is placed on larger paper with bigger print so that the cards may be seen more readily. For each concept to be taught, I have included a series of word lists so that teachers and parents may proceed more quickly with remediation. These lists are found online at http://www.prufrock.com/assets/clientpages/school-successdyslexia.aspx, and it will serve as your resource in creating your card decks. Most word lists have 20 or more words. Merely place one of the words in large print in the center of each card. I highly recommend that you use a black marker and basic print as you create your drill cards. The black print on the white background will create a contrast that aids in visual tracking.

I strongly recommend that you print the cards on cardstock (for the class set) and index cards (for the individual set). Either may be purchased at any office supply store. This will ensure that the cards will be a part of your class or home therapy operation for quite some time. As teachers and parents progress through the concepts, their stacks of drill cards will increase. Once you have your drill cards, place a rubber band around them to keep them together. Then, place them in a box large enough to index them so that you may find them quickly.

Proper Use of the Phonics Deck (Individual or Class Procedure)

Before beginning your lessons, you should create a phonics deck to use with the student.[18] The phonics deck is created in the same manner as the drill cards, but the phonemes to be studied are taken from those the student has misidentified on the Assessment of Sound-Symbol Correspondence.

At the beginning of each training session, after the writing of the cursive alphabet and long vowel spellings, take the entire phonics deck in hand and have the student orally identify the sound that the letters or phonograms make. Each card that is read appropriately should be placed on the table directly in front of you. Only cards that are read correctly and with automaticity should be classified as having been read appropriately during the diagnostic process. If a student hesitates, stammers, or mispronounces a phoneme, it constitutes inappropriate identification. Further, letters or phonograms that make multiple sounds should have the multiple sounds identified. Lack of identification of all phonemes for a single letter or phonogram also constitutes inappropriate identification if they have all been taught. Cards that are inappropriately identified should be placed to the right.

After you have exhausted the phonics deck, pick up the misidentified cards that were placed to the right. Present these cards again to the student. If the student identifies the sound that the letters or phonograms make, place the card on the table directly in front of you. Cards that are inappropriately identified should be placed to the right. Repeat this procedure until the phonics deck has been completely exhausted.

---

18   To create a phonics deck, use the Assessment of Sound-Symbol Correspondence and the same procedure for creating drill cards.

Proper Use of the Drill Cards (Class Procedure)

After a given concept has been formally introduced (see the Lesson Planning section on p. 162 for information on introducing new concepts) take the 8.5" by 11" cards for the phonogram just covered and place them in your left hand (right hand, if you are lefthanded). Hold up one card and ask the class to read aloud the card that is immediately visible. As soon as the class has successfully read the first card, place it at the bottom of the deck. If members of the class have difficulty accurately reading the word on the card, prompt the class by saying, "Look again." If members of the class continue to have difficulty accurately reading the word on the card, stop! Return the students' attention to the information that you have supplied in the student notebooks. Go over the examples that were provided for the new concept. Return to the phonogram cards only after the students demonstrate a clearer understanding of the new concept. Again, have the class read the card that is immediately visible. As soon as the class has successfully read the first card, turn it down on the table.

With this simple exercise, learning is accomplished through all three neurological pathways: visual, auditory, and tactile-kinesthetic. The individual students see the card and then hear the pronunciation of the word. Through the manipulation of the tract of articulation, the students receive tactile reinforcement as well. Because the words follow the same phonetic pattern, the class is gaining mastery over the words that follow a particular phonetic pattern.

After the deck has been exhausted for the decoding (reading), the class should be supplied with two pieces of notebook paper upon which to write. Tell the class, "Let's practice a few of these" and instruct them to take out a pencil. (Pencils provide more tactile-kinesthetic reinforcement than pens because: (a) more continuous pressure must be applied to form letters, and (b) pencils glide less. More vibration occurs while a pencil remains in contact with the paper, and stronger vibrations translate into stronger tactile-kinesthetic reinforcement.) Remind the class of the concept that you intend to practice. Turn the card deck toward you (the words should be facing you, not the class) and begin dictating the words. The procedure for the dictation of the phonogram deck for encoding purposes, in the Orton-Gillingham approach, is called Simultaneous Oral Spelling (SOS) and is as follows:

1. Clearly articulate the word in a strong, yet unobtrusive tone.

2. The class repeats the word.

3. Have the class write the word, naming each letter of the word as it is being written. (If a student prefers to say the sound that the letter or phonogram makes instead of the letter itself, this is acceptable).

4. After the class has finished writing the word, have the class look at the word and say it again.

As you move around the room during this portion of the Orton-Gillingham session, you will clearly see if the words that students are writing have been spelled correctly. If the words have been spelled correctly, place the card on the bottom of the deck and move on to dictating the next word. If you see that a student has misspelled a word, prompt the student by saying, "Take a look at what you have written." This statement should be followed by, "What are we working on?" This statement should prompt the student to make the correct adjustment. If the student continues to make errors when spelling the word, or does not remember the topic of remediation, stop! Return the student's attention to the information in the student notebook. Go over the examples that were provided for the new concept. Return to the phonogram cards only after the student demonstrates a clearer understanding of the new concept. Again, dictate the word on the card to the student. As soon as the student has successfully written the word, turn the card down on the table. Again, with this simple exercise, learning is accomplished through all three of the neurological pathways for language acquisition: auditory, visual, and tactile-kinesthetic. The student hears you say the word. The student hears her own voice repeating the word and the letters of the word while watching the formation of the letters of the word. At the same time, the student feels the movement of the pencil as it forms the letters of the word and the movement of the vocal tract as words and letters are pronounced. Finally, the student must physically see the finished word to repeat the finished word aloud. Because the words follow the same phonetic pattern, the student is gaining mastery over the words that follow a particular phonetic pattern.

The procedure for using the drill cards is a vital aspect of the Orton-Gillingham approach, and it may be adapted as reinforcement to all sorts of remediation activities, including spelling and vocabulary.

Proper Use of the Drill Cards (Individual Procedure)

After a concept has been formally introduced (see the Lesson Planning section on p. 162 for information on introducing new concepts), place yourself in a position directly across the table from the student. Take the cards for the phonogram just covered and place them in your left hand (right hand, if you are lefthanded). Ask the student to read aloud the card that is immediately visible. As soon as the student has successfully read the first card, turn it down on the table. If the student has difficulty accurately reading the word on the card, prompt the student by saying, "Look again." If the student continues to have difficulty accurately reading the word on the card, stop! Return the student's attention to the information that you have supplied in the student notebook. Go over the examples that you have written for the new concept. Return to the drill cards only after the student demonstrates a clearer understanding of the new concept. Again, have the student read the card that is immediately visible. As soon as the student has successfully read the first card, turn it down on the table. With this simple exercise, learning is accomplished through all three neurological pathways: visual, auditory, and tactile-kinesthetic. The student sees the card and then hears the pronunciation of the word. Through the manipulation of the tract of articulation, the student receives tactile reinforcement as well. Because the words follow the same phonetic pattern, the student is gaining mastery over the words that follow a particular phonetic pattern.

After the deck has been exhausted for the decoding (reading), the student should be supplied with two pieces of notebook paper upon which to write. Tell the student, "Let's practice a few of these." Provide a pencil. Pencils provide more tactile-kinesthetic reinforcement than pens because: (a) more continuous pressure must be applied to form letters and (b) pencils glide less. More vibration occurs while a pencil remains in contact with the paper, and stronger vibrations translate into stronger tactile-kinesthetic reinforcement. Remind the student of the concept that you intend to practice. Turn the card deck toward you (the words should be facing you and not the student) and begin dictating the words using Simultaneous Oral Spelling (SOS) as follows:

1.   Clearly articulate the word in a strong, yet unobtrusive tone.

2.   The student repeats the word.

3.   Have the student write the word, naming each letter of the word as it is being written. (If the student prefers to say the sound that the letter or phonogram makes instead of the letter itself, this is acceptable).

4.   After the student has finished writing the word, have the student look at the word and say it again.

From your vantage point, you will be reading the cursive word upside-down. Nevertheless, you will clearly see if the word has been spelled correctly. If the word has been spelled correctly, turn the card down on the table and move on to dictating the next word. If the word has not been spelled correctly, prompt the student by saying, "Take a look at what you have written." This statement should be followed by, "What are we working on?" If the student continues to make errors when spelling the word, or does not remember the topic of remediation, stop! Return the student's attention to the information in the student notebook. Go over the examples that you have written for the new concept. Return to the phonogram cards only after the student demonstrates a clearer understanding of the new concept. Again, dictate the word on the card to the student. As soon as the student has successfully written the word, turn the card down on the table.

With this simple exercise, learning is accomplished through all three of the neurological pathways for language acquisition: auditory, visual, and tactile-kinesthetic. The student hears you say the word. The student hears his own voice repeating the word and its letters while watching the formation of the letters of the word. At the same time, the student feels the movement of the pencil as it forms the letters of the word and the movement of the vocal tract as words and letters are pronounced. Finally, the student must physically see the finished word to repeat the finished word aloud. Because the words follow the same phonetic pattern, the student is gaining mastery over the words that follow a particular phonetic pattern.

Lesson Planning

Lesson planning is vital to the success of the Orton-Gillingham approach. To maximize the time spent with the student, the parent must have a game plan as to the constitution of the session. This is not to say that the language training session may not deviate from the game plan if necessary. In fact, it should deviate if the need arises, because one major component of the Orton-Gillingham approach is that it is diagnostic-prescriptive. Give the student only what the student requires. The lesson plan should be tailored specifically for each individual student based upon the student's level of mastery of different aspects of the English code. Although all lessons may follow a similar pattern in substance, the intricate details of the lesson application should change based upon what the student demonstrates is required.

Lesson Planning for Beginning Students

Lesson planning for the beginning student differs greatly from lesson planning for the more advanced student in many ways. First, beginning students may require more attention to the development of proper cursive writing. After the handwriting segment of the language training session is over, the student may progress at a much slower pace through the phonics deck than will an advanced student. Time must be allotted to address the proper pronunciation and development of automaticity of delivery of phonemes. The beginning student may have very little knowledge of syllabication, and the parent may have to formally introduce open, closed, and silent "e" syllables. In short, the beginning student will lack, by definition, the core components of the Orton-Gillingham approach. Therefore, I suggest that beginning students be given a session lasting 120 minutes versus the 90-minute session for advanced students or students who have been under this type of remediation for a longer time period. I make this suggestion because lesson planning for the beginning student must include the more rudimentary aspects of the approach (e.g., handwriting, pencil grip, basic syllabication, vowel sounds, consonant sounds, digraphs) that the more advanced student may readily implement.

The lesson plan for the beginning student shall include seven parts:

1. **Handwriting (10 minutes):** The student should be required to write a proper lowercase alphabet. She should sit upright in her chair with both hands on the desk or table. Feet should be flat on the floor and in front of the student. The paper upon which she is writing should be at a 45-degree angle. Time should be set aside to correct and practice

The Cursive Writing Argument

There are strong arguments not only for encouraging students to write in cursive, but also for instructing students in the proper techniques of cursive writing. Some of the more pertinent points of the cursive writing arguments are:

- Cursive writing is faster because the pen or pencil doesn't have to be lifted from the paper as often.

- There are fewer starts in cursive writing. Fewer starts translate into fewer starting points. This method of writing allows for fluid movement rather than a series of isolated strokes.

- Each lowercase letter begins on the baseline in cursive writing.

- Cursive writing greatly diminishes letter reversals. Letters that can be easily reversed (e.g., "b" and "d" or "p" and "q") not only look different, but begin in different points on the baseline.

- Cursive writing provides better kinesthetic reinforcement for automaticity and reading reinforcement.

- Utilizing the appropriate grip on the writing utensil and the appropriate positioning of the paper and the body allows students to write more legibly and for longer periods of time without fatigue.

- Words are engrained kinesthetically as units.

- The kinesthetic nature of cursive writing, along with the auditory component of simultaneous oral spelling (SOS), reinforces spelling skills.

any malformed letters. In order to correct and practice any letters that are malformed, beginning students should write on a large, vertical surface (preferably a white board or chalkboard). The cursive letters should be approximately 1 foot in size. This encourages large arm movements, increasing the amount of kinesthetic input. The parent should produce the cursive letter on the board, and the student should trace it three times. After the student has traced it three times, the student should erase the letter with the index finger of her dominant hand to trace the lines used in the creation of the letter. The student should repeat this procedure until the lines are mostly gone. Then, the parent should ask the student to recreate the letter. After the lowercase alphabet has been mastered, the student should be introduced to the uppercase letters. Time should be set aside to correct and practice any malformed letters. Immediately following the cursive handwriting, students should write the long vowel spellings for each letter in the format as demonstrated on the long vowel spelling matrix (see pp. 76–79).

2. **The Phonics Deck (15 minutes):** The parent should have an individual phonics deck for each student. As automaticity increases, the parent will remove certain graphemes and phonograms from the phonics deck. Having a phonics deck for each student makes it easier to individualize this important aspect of the language training session. Each day, the parent should take the deck in hand and ask the student to identify the phoneme that each grapheme or phonogram makes. Those that are inappropriately identified should be placed to the right of the parent. After the deck has been exhausted, the parent should pick up the cards that were inappropriately identified and represent these cards to the student for identification. If the grapheme or phoneme is inappropriately identified again, the card should be placed to the right of the parent. This procedure should be repeated until all phonograms or graphemes have been appropriately identified. This practice will take longer when the parent first begins with a student, but in time, the student will begin to automatically associate

a given grapheme or phonogram with its appropriate sound. This association is vital to the further development and translation to reading automaticity and spelling skills.

3. **Concept Review/Reading Deck (5–15 minutes):** At this point in the language training session, the parent should review the previous day's new concept. The student should be encouraged to take out the student notebook and turn to the page where the concept is located. The concept should be reviewed using the same examples written in the student notebook. The parent should then take the cards that pertain to the concept's phonogram and first use the cards as a reading deck. Ask the student to read the first card. As soon as the student has successfully read that card, turn it down on the table. If the student has difficulty accurately reading the word on the card, prompt her by saying, "Look again." If the student continues to have difficulty, stop! Return the student's attention to the information supplied in the student notebook. Go over the examples that you have written for the new concept. Return to the phonogram cards only after the student demonstrates a clearer understanding of the new concept. Again, have the student read the first card. As soon as the student has successfully read the first card, turn it down on the table. This should be completed until the deck of cards that pertains to that particular phonogram has been exhausted. After the deck has been exhausted for the reading, the student should be supplied with two pieces of notebook paper upon which to write and a pencil. Turn the card deck toward you (the words should be facing you and not the student) and begin dictating the words. The student should spell each word using Simultaneous Oral Spelling.

4. **New Concept (20 minutes):** Take the student notebook and find an appropriate page upon which to write the new concept. Concepts should be placed near similar concepts within the student notebook. (Syllable types should be placed together, long vowel spellings placed together, and so on. We don't want

the student notebook to be confusing.) The information should be written in cursive in black ink. To make the information easier to read, the parent should skip lines when writing information in the student notebook. The new concept should be clearly written at the top of the page with several examples placed beneath the explanation. The parent should then take the cards that pertain to the concept's phonogram and first use the cards as a reading deck. Ask the student to read the first card. As soon as the student has successfully read that card, turn it down on the table. If the student has difficulty accurately reading the word on the card, stop! Return the student's attention to the information supplied in the student notebook. Go over the examples that you have written for the new concept. Return to the phonogram cards only after the student demonstrates a clearer understanding of the new concept. Again, have the student read the first card. As soon as the student has successfully read the first card, turn it down on the table. This should be completed until the deck of cards that pertains to that particular phonogram has been exhausted. After the deck has been exhausted for the reading, the student should be supplied with two pieces of notebook paper upon which to write and a pencil. Turn the card deck toward you (the words should be facing you and not the student) and begin dictating the words related to the new concept. The student should spell each word using Simultaneous Oral Spelling.

5. **Spelling Pack (20 minutes):** Each student should have 25 words that present as problematic in terms of spelling. To begin, all students must be able to read and spell each and every word that appears on the Dolch Sight Word Lists (see Table 1 on p. 46). There are 220 words on the list, and they are broken down into grade levels as words that students should be able to read and spell based upon their placement in school. If students are unable to read and spell all of the words at their grade level and below, this represents a gap that must be filled before proceeding with more difficult spelling words. After students have mastered their appropriate sight words,

each should have 25 spelling words that are equivalent to his current independent reading level[19]. For example, if her current reading level is grade 5, then the spelling words should be taken from the grade 5 column of the Ayres Spelling Scale.[20] The instructor should write these spelling words on individual 3" x 5" cards. For the spelling portion of the language training session, take the spelling deck in hand, turn the deck toward you (the words should be facing you and not the student), and begin dictating the words. The student should spell each word using Simultaneous Oral Spelling. If the word is spelled correctly, place a check in the upper lefthand corner. If the word is misspelled, place an "X" in the upper lefthand corner of the card and proceed to the next card. Three checks in a row, and the card should be removed from the spelling pack and placed in a box or container designated for words with three checks.[21] Then, replace the card with a new word from the spelling scale.

6. **Grammar Concept (20 minutes):** Each language training session should involve a grammar component of some sort. The parent or teacher is to determine what this component entails based upon the academic strengths and weaknesses of the student. The ideal recommendation is to thoroughly work through the eight parts of speech. This is where I stray from the strict approach of Orton-Gillingham, which focuses solely upon the mastery of spelling rules and concepts associated with preparing a student for exposure to reading and spelling. I encourage all parents to incorporate a grammar component because part of the homework assignment (see p. 170) will consist of writing 10 sentences.

19 Determining the student's independent reading level will require the Degree of Reading Power program or a similar diagnostic program. See http://www.questarai.com/Products/DRPProgram/Pages/default.aspx for more details on this program.
20 The Ayres Spelling Scale is officially entitled *A Measuring Scale for Ability in Spelling* by Leonard Ayres. It is published by Mott Media and is available at Amazon.com.
21 At least twice a month, all cards that have been placed in the three-check box should be taken by the parent and presented to the student to spell. If the student spells the word correctly, place it back in the three-check box. If the student misspells the word, the word should be "reactivated" and placed in the student's current spelling pack.

7. **Oral Reading (10 minutes):** Each language training session should involve 10 minutes of reading aloud by the student. Oral reading is a time when the student has a chance to apply some of the spelling rules and English code conventions that were learned through language training sessions. During this time, the parent should "track" the student as he reads. Tracking is done using two techniques together. The first is for the parent to place an index card directly above the line the student is reading. The card must be directly above the line because we read from top to bottom and from left to right. We want the eyes of the student to swing freely from the end of the line to the beginning of the line beneath it. Having the card above the line being read prevents the parent from being an obstruction to this process. Secondly, in addition to the index card, the parent should track each word the student reads with a pencil, moving the pencil along the index card as each word is read. If a mistake in pronunciation has been made or a word has been inappropriately identified, the parent should stop the tracking of the pencil at the site of the error and tap the pencil tip on the index card at the error site. This signals to the student that an error of some sort has been made. There are several ways of helping a student identify an error in pronunciation. If the word is multisyllabic, the parent could divide the word into syllables. If this does not provide enough assistance to enable the student to identify the word, the parent may then pronounce the first syllable. In some cases, it may better serve the time constraint for the parent to give the student the entire pronunciation. Finally, in addition to serving as an opportunity for the student to apply some of the spelling rules and English code conventions experienced, oral reading gives the parent a chance to monitor the development of reading prosody of the student. Equally important, the parent has a chance to occasionally stop the reading and ask a comprehension question to monitor whether the student understands what is being read.

Lesson Planning for Advanced Students

The lesson plan for the advanced student shall include six parts:

1. **Handwriting (1 minute):** The student should be required to write a proper lowercase alphabet using Simultaneous Oral Spelling. The student should sit upright in the chair with both hands on the desk or table. Feet should be flat on the floor and in front of the student. The paper upon which the student is writing should be at a 45-degree angle. Time need not be set aside to correct and practice any malformed letters, because there will most likely not be any. If there are, a simple suggestion and repetition of the stroke while seated is normally enough to make the correction. Immediately following the cursive handwriting practice, students should write the long vowel spellings as demonstrated on the long vowel spelling matrix (see pp. 76–79).

2. **The Phonics Deck (14 minutes):** The phonics deck should be reviewed daily using the procedure the parent would use with a beginning student. However, because we are dealing with graphemes and phonograms that may make multiple sounds, a variation of this drill is for the parent to produce a sound and have the student write the different graphemes and phonograms that make that sound.

3. **Concept Review/Reading Deck (15 minutes):** The parent should conduct concept review as described for a beginning student.

4. **New Concept/Grammar Concept (20 minutes):** Take the student notebook and find an appropriate page upon which to write the new concept. See the lesson plans for a beginning student for more information on teaching new concepts. On some days it will be appropriate for the new concept to be a grammar concept. If the new concept is a grammar concept, no cards will be available. Instead, the parent should provide reinforcement using a grammar workbook obtained from an outside source.

5.   **Spelling Pack/Morphology Study (25 minutes):** Conduct the spelling segment as with a beginning student. The only change may be that the spelling words no longer must come from the Ayres Spelling Scale. If the parent is so inclined, the spelling words may be taken from Latinate or Greek word construction study (see Chapter 5).

6.   **Oral Reading (15 minutes):** Track oral reading as with a beginning student.

Homework Assignments

Controversially, I strongly recommend that students undergoing language remediation should only be assigned homework that relates to language development during the week. Homework that relates to math, science, and other subjects should be assigned on the weekends, when students have more time to devote to their academic endeavors. This is due to my firm belief that if students are struggling with reading, everything else is secondary. This is not an easy development to bring to pass. In my experience, each classroom is a tiny fiefdom, and each teacher feels as if his subject is most important. Even though he may understand that reading is the foundational skill of academic learning, the teacher may not wish to play "second fiddle." So, you're probably better off not dealing with the teacher directly. It won't hurt to ask, but don't hold your breath. You are better off dealing with an administrative body through the form of an IEP. There are several openings within the IEP in order to get this done. Get yourself a strong advocate and try to bring this request in under specially designed instruction, program modifications, or the extent to which the child will not participate with nondisabled children in the regular classroom. Each of these categories is federally mandated. Remember, the most fundamental responsibility of schools is to teach students how to read (Moats, 1999). Additionally, the development of reading skills obviously serves as the gateway to the world of printed information, as reading skill serves as the major foundational skill for all school-based learning (Lyon, 1998a). Reading comes first.

Weekday assignments for students that relate to language development should contain, at the minimum, six components, depending upon the age of the student: reinforcement of phonics concepts, reading comprehension, sentence writing, spelling packs, oral reading, and, if the student is the fourth grade or higher, morphology study.

Reinforcement of Phonics/Grammar

Language training concepts need to be enforced if they are to take root in the minds of our students. For example, when presented with vc/cv syllable division, students will need to practice this syllable division outside of class or the language training session. There are two resources that will prove invaluable as you proceed with language training concepts. The first is *Solving Language Difficulties: Remedial Routines*, a book by written by Amey Steere, Caroline Z. Peck, and Linda Kahn. It is an invaluable resource available from Educators Publishing Service. This single resource allows you to reinforce the following:

- the seven syllable types,
- syllable division,
- the accent,
- the schwa,
- the three sounds of "-ed,"
- the seven spelling rules, and
- the three sounds of "y."

The second resource is *The Spell of Words,* a book by written by Elsie T. Rak. This, too, is an invaluable resource available from Educators Publishing Service. This single resource allows you to reinforce the following:

- the two sounds of "c," "g," and "s";

- "r"-controlled spellings;

- vowel teams; and

- diphthongs.

In addition to needing reinforcement of language training concepts (e.g., syllable division, the long spelling rule), students will need reinforcement for the grammatical concepts that are an integral part of language training. An excellent resource for reinforcing grammar skills is *Exercises in English Grammar* by John H. Treanor. This resource is available on Amazon.

Reading Comprehension

To foster and reinforce proper reading comprehension skills, I recommend the Six-Way Paragraphs books by Dr. Walter Pauk. The three books in the series are available online from Amazon. Using Dr. Pauk's series, students will improve reading comprehension through the mastery of the following six essential categories:

- main idea,

- supporting details,

- clarifying devices,

- inference,

- drawing conclusions, and

- vocabulary in context.

Sentence Writing

The number of times the sentences should be written is equal to the number of language training sessions per week. If there are three sessions per week, the beginning student should write 10 sentences three nights per week, preferably the night after a language training session. Advanced students should write 20–30 sentences for each day of language training. Sentences should be based upon the words found within the student's spelling pack or morphology pack (for older, more advanced students). These words should be underlined and spelled/used correctly. During the construction of the sentences, students should be encouraged to strictly follow the rules for sentence construction (e.g., agreement, punctuation).

In essence, writing sentences every night serves as constant practice in the usage and application of the English code because:

- Students must remember and apply basic to advanced rules for capitalization and punctuation.

- Students must remember and apply basic to advanced rules for subjects and predicates.

- Students must be conscious of proper sentence structure.

- An advanced form of sentence writing incorporates the usage of spelling words in the nightly sentences. Therefore, students must know how to use the spelling words they have been given. This increases vocabulary development.

- Depending upon the level of the student, the 10 sentences may be simple, compound, complex, or compound-complex. In either case, from the compound sentences through compound-complex sentences, the students must also be aware of the conventions involved in the proper use of coordinating and subordinating conjunctions as well as dependent and independent clauses.

Spelling

Each spelling word that is in the student's spelling pack[22] should be written in cursive in order to reinforce the correct spelling of the word. The words should be written using the following pattern as a guideline:

- If the word is new or has an "X" for the student's last attempt at spelling it, write it four times each.

- If the word has one check, write it three times each.

- If the word has two checks, write it two times each.

The student should have the card sitting directly in front of him as the word is being written *and* should write the word using Simultaneous Oral Spelling.

Oral Reading

This is a private reading time. The student should read aloud for a minimum of 10 minutes at home. This reading should take place within earshot of the parent. This is important. Students with reading difficulty will frequently look at the first few letters of a word and say the first word that comes to their minds with a close letter sequence (e.g., "prerogative" may be pronounced "program"), and the student will just keep going. If the parent is within earshot, he or she will know whether the pronounced words actually fit in the sentence based upon context.

In order for parents and other specialists to accurately determine the reading level of their students, I highly recommend the *Degree of Reading Power* (DRP) program, a highly effective, yet relatively inexpensive program by Questar Assessment, Inc. (http://www.questarai.com). The DRP program offers a diagnostic test that may be administered by parents at home or by teachers in a classroom setting.

---

22 These words may be taken from the Dolch Sight Words Lists, the Ayres Spelling Scale, or vocabulary words based upon Latinate or Greek word constructions.

Based upon the performance on the test, students earn two scores: an instructional DRP score and an independent DRP score. The instructional DRP score indicates the most difficult text a student can read and understand with teachers' or parents' help. The independent DRP score indicates the most difficult text a student can read and understand without teachers' or parents' help. Our interests lie with the independent DRP score.

Questar Assessment, Inc. has a database containing more than 36,000 titles that have been organized based upon text difficulty and assigned a number that corresponds to the independent DRP scores. Simply type in your student's independent DRP score, and you are presented with a detailed and comprehensive list of titles of books at your child's independent reading level. Parents and other specialists will have no difficulty in finding these books at their local public library or online at Amazon. Then, students can choose from the books at their independent reading levels for oral reading time.

Morphology

Each student in the fourth grade or higher who receives language remediation must be involved in morphology study. Morphology is the study of Latinate and Greek word constructions and their influences upon the English vocabulary. Remember that the preponderance of the English language is composed of Latinate word construction (55%), Anglo-Saxon word construction (25%), and Greek word construction (11%). Therefore, the ability to recognize and manipulate the various prefixes, suffixes, roots, and combining forms is important to strengthening visual and auditory processing abilities. Students encounter Anglo-Saxon words from the very beginning of their academic careers. They begin their exposure to Latinate word construction in approximately the fourth grade, and to Greek word construction in middle school. Familiarizing your student with Latinate and Greek word constructions proves to be extremely important, because between the two, they comprise 66% of the words in the English code. That is two out of every three words.

Parents may make their own morphology (Latinate prefixes and roots/Greek combining forms) cards based upon the Greek combining forms and the Latinate roots and affixes found in the appendices of this work. The suggested layout of the back of the card is shown in Figure 21.

As you may imagine, the method for proceeding is more challenging if the student is in middle school and is just now beginning language remediation. Not only will she have to master Greek word construction, but she will also have to master the Anglo-Saxon and Latinate word constructions that come before it. In either case, you may begin with a rudimentary discussion regarding word construction.[23]

Whether you are introducing Latinate roots or prefixes or Greek combining forms, the procedure is the same. I recommend having your child memorize three at a time. She should be able to recite the root, the meaning, and a keyword listed on three of the cards without looking on the back of any card. After she has memorized the three cards, place them aside. Grab three more. She should memorize this group of three until she can recite the root, the meaning, and a keyword without looking on the back. Then, pick up the previous group of three, and review all six. The student should be able to recite the root, the meaning, and a keyword for all six without looking on the back of any card. Once she is able to do this, place the group of six cards aside. Grab three more cards. The student should memorize this group of three until she can recite the root, the meaning, and a keyword without looking on the back. Then, pick up the previous group of six cards, and review all nine of them. The student should be able to recite the root, the meaning, and a keyword for all nine without looking on the back of any card. Once she is able to do this, place the group of nine cards aside, and grab three more. Allow this group of 12 to settle within the child's mind for a couple of days.

For students studying Latinate word construction, have them memorize 21 roots and 21 prefixes. Once they have demonstrated mastery of this group, have them create various real words using the prefixes and roots. When you feel comfortable, have them repeat the

---

23   Refer to the chapter on English Language Word Construction (Chapter 5) and begin accordingly.

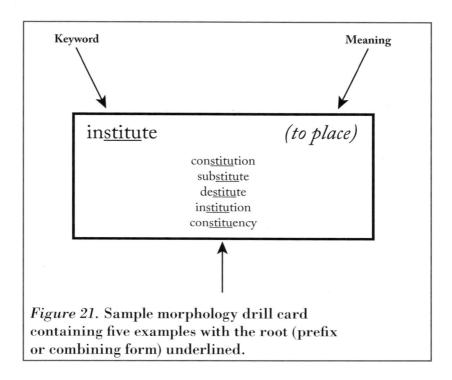

Figure 21. Sample morphology drill card containing five examples with the root (prefix or combining form) underlined.

process of "three at a time" as they master 21 more Latinate roots. Students should have mastery of at least 50 Latinate roots before parents attempt to teach the assimilated Latinate prefixes.

For those studying Greek word construction, have them repeat the process of "three at a time" until they have mastered 45 Greek combining forms. Have them create words using the Greek combining forms (don't forget the connective "o"). When you feel comfortable, have them repeat the process of "three at a time" as they master successive groups of Greek combining forms.

Chapter Summary

The provision of academic language therapy helps students who need primary instruction or remediation with the English code. Because the educational experience of American students is conducted primarily in the English language, adequate language skills are essential for school success. The aforementioned strategies are those that may be done at home or in the classroom by a dedicated individual to aid in remediation during these financially trying times.

References

American Psychiatric Association. (2000). *Diagnostic and statistical manual of mental disorders* (4th ed., Text Rev.). Washington, DC: Author.

Barton, S. (2011). *Adult literacy.* Retrieved from http://www.bartonreading.com/pdf/pages/Barton_Adult_Literacy.pdf

Edmonds, M., Vaughn, S., Wexler, J., Reutebuch, C., Cable, A., Tackett, K., & Schnakenberg, J. W. (2009). A synthesis of reading interventions and effects on reading comprehension outcomes for older struggling readers. *Review of Educational Research, 79,* 262–300.

Fromkin, V., Hyams, N., & Rodman, R. (2002). *An introduction to language.* Fort Worth, TX: Harcourt Brace Jovanovich.

Georgia Project for Assistive Technology. (n.d.). *Contrast aids.* Retrieved from http://www.gpat.org/Georgia-Project-for-Assistive-Technology/Pages/Contrast-Aids.aspx

Individuals with Disabilities Education Improvement Act, Pub. Law 108-446 (December 3, 2004).

International Dyslexia Association. (2008). *Just the facts.* Retrieved from http://www.interdys.org

K12 Reader. (n.d.). *Teaching sight words: Effective strategies for reading success.* Retrieved from http://www.k12reader.com/sight-word-teaching-strategies

LDOnline. (2010). *What is a learning disability?* Retrieved from http://www.ldonline.org/ldbasics/whatisld

Learning Inside-Out. (n.d.). *Dyslexia statistics.* Retrieved from http://www.learning-inside-out.com/dyslexia-statistics.html

Learning Points Associates. (2004). *A closer look at the five essential components of effective reading instruction.* Retrieved from http://www.learningpt.org/pdfs/literacy/components.pdf

Loury, G. C., & Western, B. (2010, Summer). The challenge of mass incarceration in America. *Journal of the American Academy of the Arts and Sciences, 8–19.*

Lyon, G. R. (1998a). *Overview of reading and literacy initiatives: Testimony before a United States Senate committee on labor and human resources.* Retrieved from http://www.reidlyon.com/edpolicy/5-OVERVIEW-OF-READING-AND-LITERACY-INITIATIVES.pdf

Lyon, G. R. (1998b, March). Why reading is not a natural process. *Educational Leadership, 14–18.*

May, T. (2006). *BrainWork.* New York, NY: The Dana Foundation.

Moats, L. (1999). *Teaching reading is rocket science.* Washington, DC: American Federation of Teachers.

Myomancy. (2005). *Auditory processing disorder and dyslexia.* Retrieved from http://www.myomancy.com/2005/08/auditory_proces

Pew Center on the States. (2008). *One in 100: Behind bars in America 2008.* Retrieved from http://www.angola3.org/uploads/Pew-Report-0208.pdf

Reading Rockets. (2012). *Text comprehension.* Retrieved from http://www.readingrockets.org/teaching/reading101/comprehension

Section 504 of the Rehabilitation Act, 29 U.S.C. Section 706 et. Seq. (1973).

appendix A

Scripts for Teaching Segmenting and Rhyming

NOTE that students will likely find other words that rhyme with those in the scripts. The words included are simply a guide for parents to follow.

Teacher/Parent Instruction	Expected Student Answer
Say "spill."	"spill"
Sound it out for me.	/s/ /p/ /ĭ/ /l/
How many sounds are in the word "spill"?	Four
How many syllables?	One
How many digraphs?	One
How many blends?	One
How many clusters?	Zero
Give me five words that rhyme with "spill."	bill, dill, fill, gill, mill

Teacher/Parent Instruction	Expected Student Answer
Say "strap."	"strap"
Sound it out for me.	/s/ /t/ /r/ /ă/ /p/
How many sounds are in the word "strap"?	Five
How many syllables?	One
How many digraphs?	Zero
How many blends?	Zero
How many clusters?	One
Give me five words that rhyme with "strap."	cap, lap, gap, nap, wrap

Teacher/Parent Instruction	Expected Student Answer
Say "sail."	"sail"
Sound it out for me.	/s/ /ā/ /l/
How many sounds are in the word "sail"?	Three
How many syllables?	One
How many digraphs?	Zero
How many blends?	Zero
How many clusters?	Zero
Give me five words that rhyme with "sail."	hail, mail, tail, pail, rail

Teacher/Parent Instruction	Expected Student Answer
Say "box."	"box"
Sound it out for me.	/ b / / ŏ / / k / / s /
How many sounds are in the word "box"?	Four
How many syllables?	One
How many digraphs?	Zero
How many blends?	Zero
How many clusters?	Zero
Give me five words that rhyme with "box."	ox, fox, lox, stocks, socks

Teacher/Parent Instruction	Expected Student Answer
Say "spring."	"spring"
Sound it out for me.	/ s / / p / / r / / ĭ / / n / / g /
How many sounds are in the word "spring"?	Five
How many syllables?	One
How many digraphs?	Zero
How many blends?	One
How many clusters?	One
Give me five words that rhyme with "spring."	sing, bring, thing, string, zing

Teacher/Parent Instruction	Expected Student Answer
Say "bug."	"bug"
Sound it out for me.	/ b / / ŭ / / g /
How many sounds are in the word "bug"?	Three
How many syllables?	One
How many digraphs?	Zero
How many blends?	Zero
How many clusters?	Zero
Give me five words that rhyme with "bug."	dug, chug, lug, hug, tug

Teacher/Parent Instruction	Expected Student Answer
Say "dock."	"dock"
Sound it out for me.	/ d / / ŏ / / k /
How many sounds are in the word "dock"?	Three
How many syllables?	One
How many digraphs?	One
How many blends?	Zero
How many clusters?	Zero
Give me five words that rhyme with "dock."	block, lock, jock, mock, knock

Teacher/Parent Instruction	Expected Student Answer
Say "truck."	"truck"
Sound it out for me.	/ t / / r / / ŭ / / k /
How many sounds are in the word "truck"?	Four
How many syllables?	One
How many digraphs?	One
How many blends?	One
How many clusters?	Zero
Give me five words that rhyme with "truck."	buck, duck, luck, muck, puck

Teacher/Parent Instruction	Expected Student Answer
Say "slack."	"slack"
Sound it out for me.	/ s / / l / / ă / / k /
How many sounds are in the word "slack"?	Three
How many syllables?	One
How many digraphs?	One
How many blends?	One
How many clusters?	Zero
Give me five words that rhyme with "slack."	back, lack, hack, tack, sack

Teacher/Parent Instruction	Expected Student Answer
Say "sham."	"sham"
Sound it out for me.	/ sh / / ă / / m /
How many sounds are in the word "sham"?	Three
How many syllables?	One
How many digraphs?	One
How many blends?	Zero
How many clusters?	Zero
Give me five words that rhyme with "sham."	ram, cram, am, gram, ham

Teacher/Parent Instruction	Expected Student Answer
Say "grass."	"grass"
Sound it out for me.	/ g / / r / / ă / / s /
How many sounds are in the word "grass"?	Four
How many syllables?	One
How many digraphs?	One
How many blends?	One
How many clusters?	Zero
Give me five words that rhyme with "grass."	bass, class, gas, mass, pass

Teacher/Parent Instruction	Expected Student Answer
Say "trod."	"trod"
Sound it out for me.	/ t / / r / / ŏ / / d /
How many sounds are in the word "trod"?	Four
How many syllables?	One
How many digraphs?	Zero
How many blends?	One
How many clusters?	Zero
Give me five words that rhyme with "trod."	cod, rod, nod, pod, sod

Teacher/Parent Instruction	Expected Student Answer
Say "slot."	"slot"
Sound it out for me.	/ s / / l / / ŏ / / t /
How many sounds are in the word "slot"?	Four
How many syllables?	One
How many digraphs?	Zero
How many blends?	One
How many clusters?	Zero
Give me five words that rhyme with "slot."	cot, dot, got, hot, pot

Teacher/Parent Instruction	Expected Student Answer
Say "tent."	"tent"
Sound it out for me.	/ t / / ĕ / / n / / t /
How many sounds are in the word "tent"?	Four
How many syllables?	One
How many digraphs?	Zero
How many blends?	One
How many clusters?	Zero
Give me five words that rhyme with "tent."	bent, sent, rent, lent, meant

Teacher/Parent Instruction	Expected Student Answer
Say "wet."	"wet"
Sound it out for me.	/ w / / ĕ / / t /
How many sounds are in the word "wet"?	Three
How many syllables?	One
How many digraphs?	Zero
How many blends?	Zero
How many clusters?	Zero
Give me five words that rhyme with "wet."	bet, let, get, met, debt

Teacher/Parent Instruction	Expected Student Answer
Say "dab."	"dab"
Sound it out for me.	/ d / / ă / / b /
How many sounds are in the word "dab"?	Three
How many syllables?	One
How many digraphs?	Zero
How many blends?	Zero
How many clusters?	Zero
Give me five words that rhyme with "dab."	cab, gab, nab, tab, drab

Teacher/Parent Instruction	Expected Student Answer
Say "mad."	"mad"
Sound it out for me.	/ m / / ă / / d /
How many sounds are in the word "mad"?	Three
How many syllables?	One
How many digraphs?	Zero
How many blends?	Zero
How many clusters?	Zero
Give me five words that rhyme with "mad."	bad, sad, had, dad, glad

Teacher/Parent Instruction	Expected Student Answer
Say "dust."	"dust"
Sound it out for me.	/ d / / ŭ / / s / / t /
How many sounds are in the word "dust"?	Four
How many syllables?	One
How many digraphs?	Zero
How many blends?	One
How many clusters?	Zero
Give me five words that rhyme with "dust."	bust, gust, fussed, rust, must

Teacher/Parent Instruction	Expected Student Answer
Say "west."	"west"
Sound it out for me.	/ w / / ĕ / / s / / t /
How many sounds are in the word "west"?	Four
How many syllables?	One
How many digraphs?	Zero
How many blends?	One
How many clusters?	Zero
Give me five words that rhyme with "west."	best, rest, test, dressed, nest

Teacher/Parent Instruction	Expected Student Answer
Say "lid."	"lid"
Sound it out for me.	/ l / / ĭ / / d /
How many sounds are in the word "lid"?	Three
How many syllables?	One
How many digraphs?	Zero
How many blends?	Zero
How many clusters?	Zero
Give me five words that rhyme with "lid."	bid, did, hid, grid, rid

Teacher/Parent Instruction	Expected Student Answer
Say "splash."	"splash"
Sound it out for me.	/ s / / p / / l / / ă / / sh /
How many sounds are in the word "splash"?	Five
How many syllables?	One
How many digraphs?	One
How many blends?	Zero
How many clusters?	One
Give me five words that rhyme with "splash."	bash, sash, hash, gash, mash

Teacher/Parent Instruction	Expected Student Answer
Say "most."	"most"
Sound it out for me.	/ m / / ō / / s / / t /
How many sounds are in the word "most"?	Four
How many syllables?	One
How many digraphs?	Zero
How many blends?	One
How many clusters?	Zero
Give me five words that rhyme with "most."	boast, coast, ghost, post, host

Teacher/Parent Instruction	Expected Student Answer
Say "spread."	"spread"
Sound it out for me.	/ s / / p / / r / / ĕ / / d /
How many sounds are in the word "spread"?	Five
How many syllables?	One
How many digraphs?	Zero
How many blends?	Zero
How many clusters?	One
Give me five words that rhyme with "spread."	bed, head, dead, red, said

Teacher/Parent Instruction	Expected Student Answer
Say "rum."	"rum"
Sound it out for me.	/ r / / ŭ / / m /
How many sounds are in the word "rum"?	Three
How many syllables?	One
How many digraphs?	Zero
How many blends?	Zero
How many clusters?	Zero
Give me five words that rhyme with "rum."	bum, come, hum, drum, sum

Teacher/Parent Instruction	Expected Student Answer
Say "stop."	"stop"
Sound it out for me.	$/s//t//\breve{o}//p/$
How many sounds are in the word "stop"?	Four
How many syllables?	One
How many digraphs?	Zero
How many blends?	One
How many clusters?	Zero
Give me five words that rhyme with "stop."	mop, pop, hop, drop, crop

Teacher/Parent Instruction	Expected Student Answer
Say "strand."	"strand"
Sound it out for me.	$/s//t//r//\breve{a}//n//d/$
How many sounds are in the word "strand"?	Six
How many syllables?	One
How many digraphs?	Zero
How many blends?	One
How many clusters?	One
Give me five words that rhyme with "strand."	and, band, sand, hand, fanned

Teacher/Parent Instruction	Expected Student Answer
Say "mob."	"mob"
Sound it out for me.	$/m//\breve{o}//b/$
How many sounds are in the word "mob"?	Three
How many syllables?	One
How many digraphs?	Zero
How many blends?	Zero
How many clusters?	Zero
Give me five words that rhyme with "mob."	bob, cob, lob, job, rob

Teacher/Parent Instruction	Expected Student Answer
Say "drip."	"drip"
Sound it out for me.	/ d / / r / / ĭ / / p /
How many sounds are in the word "drip"?	Four
How many syllables?	One
How many digraphs?	Zero
How many blends?	One
How many clusters?	Zero
Give me five words that rhyme with "drip."	clip, lip, hip, trip, sip

Teacher/Parent Instruction	Expected Student Answer
Say "cut."	"cut"
Sound it out for me.	/ k / / ŭ / / t /
How many sounds are in the word "cut"?	Three
How many syllables?	One
How many digraphs?	Zero
How many blends?	Zero
How many clusters?	Zero
Give me five words that rhyme with "cut."	gut, hut, putt, rut, nut

Teacher/Parent Instruction	Expected Student Answer
Say "fell."	"fell"
Sound it out for me.	/ f / / ĕ / / l /
How many sounds are in the word "fell"?	Three
How many syllables?	One
How many digraphs?	Zero
How many blends?	Zero
How many clusters?	Zero
Give me five words that rhyme with "fell."	bell, dell, tell, sell, well

Teacher/Parent Instruction	Expected Student Answer
Say "sick."	"sick"
Sound it out for me.	/ s / / ĭ / / k /
How many sounds are in the word "sick"?	Three
How many syllables?	One
How many digraphs?	One
How many blends?	Zero
How many clusters?	Zero
Give me five words that rhyme with "sick."	lick, nick, trick, brick, slick

Teacher/Parent Instruction	Expected Student Answer
Say "skid."	"skid"
Sound it out for me.	/ s / / k / / ĭ / / d /
How many sounds are in the word "skid"?	Four
How many syllables?	One
How many digraphs?	Zero
How many blends?	One
How many clusters?	Zero
Give me five words that rhyme with "skid."	bid, hid, lid, rid, did

Teacher/Parent Instruction	Expected Student Answer
Say "bud."	"bud"
Sound it out for me.	/ b / / ŭ / / d /
How many sounds are in the word "bud"?	Three
How many syllables?	One
How many digraphs?	Zero
How many blends?	Zero
How many clusters?	Zero
Give me five words that rhyme with "bud."	cud, dud, mud, blood, stud

Teacher/Parent Instruction	Expected Student Answer
Say "fun."	"fun"
Sound it out for me.	/f/ /ŭ/ /n/
How many sounds are in the word "fun"?	Three
How many syllables?	One
How many digraphs?	Zero
How many blends?	Zero
How many clusters?	Zero
Give me five words that rhyme with "fun."	bun, done, gun, pun, nun

Teacher/Parent Instruction	Expected Student Answer
Say "win."	"win"
Sound it out for me.	/w/ /ĭ/ /n/
How many sounds are in the word "win"?	Three
How many syllables?	One
How many digraphs?	Zero
How many blends?	Zero
How many clusters?	Zero
Give me five words that rhyme with "win."	sin, tin, chin, bin, fin

Teacher/Parent Instruction	Expected Student Answer
Say "ate."	"ate"
Sound it out for me.	/ā/ /t/
How many sounds are in the word "ate"?	Two
How many syllables?	One
How many digraphs?	Zero
How many blends?	Zero
How many clusters?	Zero
Give me five words that rhyme with "ate."	bait, date, rate, wait, fate

Teacher/Parent Instruction	Expected Student Answer
Say "drag."	"drag"
Sound it out for me.	/d/ /r/ /ă/ /g/
How many sounds are in the word "drag"?	Four
How many syllables?	One
How many digraphs?	Zero
How many blends?	One
How many clusters?	Zero
Give me five words that rhyme with "drag."	bag, hag, gag, lag, nag

Phoneme Deletion/ Substitution Drills

Ask students to make the directed alterations to the following words.

Say "drag."
Change the last sound to / *b* /.   drab

Say "stripe."
Say "stripe" without the / *s* /.   tripe

Say "flush."
Change the vowel sound to / *ă* /.   flash

Say "loan."
Change the vowel sound to / *ī* /.   line

Say "reach."
Change the first sound to / *b* /.   beach

Say "toast."
Change the vowel sound to / ĕ /.   test

Say "flip."
Change the first sound to / k /.   clip

Say "spin."
Say "spin" without the / s /.   pin

Say "trap."
Change the last sound to / k /.   track

Say "duct."
Say "duct" without the / t /.   duck

Say "bench."
Change the vowel sound to / ŭ /.   bunch

Say "brig."
Change the vowel sound to / ă /.   brag

Say "bang."
Change the first sound to / r /.   rang

Say "spit."
Change the last sound to / n /.   spin

Say "held."
Change the vowel sound to / ō /.   hold

Say "wept."
Say "wept" without the / p /.   wet

Say "smelt."
Change the last sound to / d /.   smelled

Say "drum."
Say "drum" without the / *d* /.   rum

Say "help".
Change the last sound to / *d* /.   held

Say "snap."
Say "snap" without the / *n* /.   sap

Say "self."
Change the first sound to / *sh* /.   shelf

Say "left."
Say "left" without the / *f* /.   let

Say "desk."
Change the vowel sound to / *ĭ* /.   disk

Say "silk."
Say "silk" without the / *l* /.   sick

Say "yelp."
Change the first sound to / *h* /.   help

Say "pill."
Change the first sound to the last sound
and the last sound to the first sound.   lip

Say "map."
Change the first sound to the last sound
and the last sound to the first sound.   Pam

Say "perch."
Change the first sound to the last sound
and the last sound to the first sound.   chirp

Say "chip."
Change the first sound to the last sound
and the last sound to the first sound.   pitch

Say "lap."
Change the first sound to the last sound
and the last sound to the first sound.   pal

Say "toke."
Change the first sound to the last sound
and the last sound to the first sound.   coat

Say "mile."
Change the first sound to the last sound
and the last sound to the first sound.   lime

Say "pass."
Change the first sound to the last sound
and the last sound to the first sound.   sap

Say "law."
Change the first sound to the last sound
and the last sound to the first sound.   all

Say "kite."
Change the first sound to the last sound
and the last sound to the first sound.   tike

Say "curl."
Change the first sound to the last sound
and the last sound to the first sound.   lurk

appendix C   Latinate Roots

Root	Meaning	Examples	
annu, enni	year	annual perennial bicentennial	semiannual centennial annuity
aqua, aque	water	aquarium aquatic aqueduct	aqueous aquamarine aquanaut
aud	to hear	audience audible audit	auditory audition auditorium
ben, bon	good	benefit benign benefactor	bonus bonanza
cad, cas, cid	to fall	cadaver casualty deciduous	incident decadence occasion
ced, ceed, cess	to go	exceed procedure intercession	antecedent succeed recess
cept, ceit, ceiv	to take	reception conceit conceive	receive perceptive intercept
cis	to cut	precise excise incisor	incision precision decisive
claim, clam	to declare	exclaim acclaim proclaim	proclamation exclamation disclaimer

Root	Meaning	Examples	
clud, clus	to shut	in**clude**	con**clus**ion
		ex**clude**	se**clude**
		ex**clus**ive	con**clus**ive
corp	body	**corp**oration	**corp**oreal
		corporal	in**corp**oration
		corpulent	**corp**se
cour, cord	heart	**cour**age	**cour**ageous
		ac**cord**	**cour**teous
		en**cour**age	**cord**ial
cred	to believe	**cred**it	**cred**itor
		in**cred**ible	dis**cred**it
		credential	in**cred**ulous
crim	to offend	**crim**inal	in**crim**inate
		criminalization	dis**crim**inate
		criminologist	dis**crim**ination
cur	to run	**cur**rent	**cur**sory
		oc**cur**	ex**cur**sion
		currency	**cur**sive
dic, dict	to say	**dict**ionary	de**dic**ate
		in**dic**ate	vale**dict**orian
		dictator	pre**dict**
dom	to rule	**dom**inant	**dom**inance
		dominion	**dom**ination
		in**dom**itable	pre**dom**inance
duc, duct	to lead	pro**duct**ion	intro**duce**
		ab**duct**	re**duce**
		pro**duce**	pro**duct**ion
fact, fict, fect	to make	**fact**ory	manu**fact**ure
		factual	con**fect**ion
		fiction	in**fect**ed
fer	to carry	trans**fer**	con**fer**ence
		dif**fer**ent	re**fer**ral
		re**fer**ence	de**fer**
fid, fed	trust	**fed**eral	**fid**elity
		con**fid**ence	**fed**eration
		con**fed**erate	**fid**uciary

Root	Meaning	Examples	
fin	to end	infinite	finance
		define	refine
		finalize	confinement
fix	to fasten	fixture	prefix
		suffix	transfix
		fixation	fixate
flex, flect	to bend	reflect	deflect
		flexible	flexibility
		reflector	inflection
forc, fort	to strengthen	forceful	effortless
		fortify	comfort
		enforce	comfortable
frag, fract	to break	fragment	fraction
		fracture	fragmentation
		fragile	infraction
fus	to pour	confuse	confusion
		refuse	refusal
		profuse	infusion
grad, gress	to step	progress	aggressive
		congress	gradually
		graduate	regress
greg	flock together	congregation	egregious
		aggregate	congregate
		segregate	gregarious
her, hes	to stick	adhesive	inherent
		coherent	incoherent
		adhesion	cohesive
ject	to throw	eject	projector
		reject	conjecture
		subject	trajectory
join, joint, junct	to join	junction	disjointed
		conjoin	adjunct
		conjunction	conjunctivitis
lect	to choose	collect	delectable
		elect	predilection
		select	election

Root	Meaning	Examples	
leg	law	**leg**al **leg**acy il**leg**al	**leg**islate **leg**islature **leg**ation
loc	to place	**loc**ation **loc**al dis**loc**ate	**loc**omotion al**loc**ate **loc**alize
loqu	talk, speech	e**loqu**ent col**loqu**ial e**loqu**ence	soli**loqu**y ventri**loqu**ist col**loqu**ium
lud, lus	to play, to mock	il**lus**ion il**lus**ory de**lud**e	pre**lud**e col**lud**e col**lus**ion
mand, mend	to order	recom**mend** de**mand** **mand**ate	com**mand**ment com**mend**ation recom**mend**ation
mem	to remember	**mem**ory **mem**orandum com**mem**orate	**mem**orable **mem**orize **mem**orial
merg, mers	to sink	im**mers**e e**merg**e **merg**er	**merg**e im**mers**ion sub**mers**e
mit, mis	to send	trans**mit** per**mis**sion sub**mit**	de**mis**e pro**mis**e inter**mit**tent
mort	death	**mort**al im**mort**al **mort**ification	**mort**ician **mort**ify **mort**uary
mut	to change	**mut**ant **mut**ation **mut**ual	trans**mut**e im**mut**able com**mut**er
nat	birth	**nat**ure **nat**ion **nat**al	super**nat**ural **nat**ive inter**nat**ional
nov	new	**nov**el **nov**a **nov**elty	**nov**ice re**nov**ate in**nov**ative

Root	Meaning	Examples	
nunci, nounc	to declare, warn	de**nounce**	**announc**er
		e**nunci**ate	**announc**ement
		pro**nunci**ation	pro**nounce**
pel, puls	to drive	pro**pel**ler	re**pel**lant
		com**puls**ive	im**puls**e
		pro**puls**ion	ex**pel**
pend, pens	to hang	**pend**ulum	com**pens**ate
		de**pend**	ex**pend**iture
		sus**pens**e	sus**pens**ion
ply, plic	to fold	multi**ply**	ex**plic**it
		ap**plic**able	im**plic**ate
		sup**ply**	multi**ply**
port	to carry	**port**able	re**port**er
		trans**port**ation	sup**port**ive
		dispro**port**ionate	·de**port**ation
pos, posit	to place	**posit**ion	de**posit**
		de**pos**e	pre**posit**ion
		com**pos**er	pro**pos**al
quir, quis, quest	to ask	**quest**ion	prere**quis**ite
		in**quir**e	in**quis**ition
		re**quir**ement	re**quir**e
reg, rect	straight, lead	**reg**ular	**reg**ular
		di**rect**or	**rect**angle
		regent	**reg**ulate
rog	to question	inter**rog**ate	ar**rog**ant
		inter**rog**ation	pre**rog**ative
		de**rog**ative	sur**rog**ate
rupt	to break	e**rupt**ion	**rupt**ure
		ab**rupt**	inter**rupt**ion
		cor**rupt**	dis**rupt**
scrib, script	to write	**script**ure	**scrib**ble
		sub**script**ion	**script**ure
		pre**scrib**e	circum**scrib**e
sent, sens	to feel	re**sent**	**sent**iment
		con**sent**	**sent**inel
		sensory	in**sens**itive

Root	Meaning	Examples	
serv	to keep	preserve	reserve
		conserve	reservation
		conservative	deserve
sid	to sit, to settle	reside	president
		resident	dissident
		consider	preside
sist	to stand	assist	consistency
		consist	assistance
		resistor	persistence
solv, solut, solu	to loosen, to free	solvent	solution
		resolve	soluble
		dissolve	resolution
son	sound	consonant	resonate
		hypersonic	assonance
		sonic	dissonance
spic, spec, spect	to see	spectator	suspect
		conspicuous	special
		despicable	suspicion
spir	to breathe	perspiration	conspiracy
		spiritual	transpire
		respirator	spirit
spond, spons	to answer	respond	sponsor
		correspond	responsible
		response	correspondent
stant, stanc	to stand	instant	substantial
		constant	instantaneous
		distance	substance
stitu	to place	institute	destitute
		constitution	institution
		substitute	constituency
strict	to bind, to tighten	restriction	constriction
		district	restricted
		restrict	
struct	to build	structure	instructor
		construction	obstruct
		destruction	instruction

Root	Meaning	Examples	
tact, tang	to touch	**tang**ential	**tact**ics
		tactile	**tang**ent
		tactician	**tang**ible
tend, tens, tent	to stretch	ex**tend**	con**tent**ion
		ex**tens**ion	in**tent**
		tension	con**tend**er
test	to witness	**test**ify	con**test**
		testimony	pro**test**
		testament	at**test**
tin, ten, tain	to hold	con**tain**er	con**tin**ent
		ob**tain**	sus**ten**ance
		de**ten**tion	enter**tain**
tort	to twist	con**tort**	re**tort**
		dis**tort**	con**tort**ionist
		torture	dis**tort**ion
tract	to pull	**tract**or	at**tract**ive
		con**tract**	**tract**ion
		sub**tract**ion	dis**tract**ion
trib	to give	**trib**ute	dis**trib**ute
		at**trib**ute	**trib**utary
		con**trib**ute	re**trib**ution
trud, trus	to push	in**trud**er	in**trus**ion
		pro**trus**ion	in**trus**ive
		pro**trud**e	ob**trud**e
vac	empty	**vac**ancy	e**vac**uate
		vacate	**vac**ation
		vacant	**vac**uous
ven, vent	to come	in**vent**	pre**vent**
		con**vent**ion	ad**vent**ure
		in**vent**ion	inter**ven**e
vers, vert	to turn	re**vers**e	sub**vers**ion
		di**vert**	**vert**ebrate
		ad**vert**ise	**vers**atile
vict, vinc	to conquer	**vict**im	con**vinc**e
		con**vict**	in**vinc**ible
		victory	e**vict**ion

Root	Meaning	Examples	
vis, vid	to see	**vis**ion	e**vid**ence
		re**vis**ion	pro**vid**e
		visa	e**vid**ent
voc, vok	to call	pro**vok**e	in**voc**ation
		ad**voc**ate	equi**voc**ate
		in**vok**e	**voc**alize
volv, volut	to roll	e**volv**e	re**volv**e
		re**volut**ion	e**volut**ion
		in**volv**e	in**volv**ement

Latinate Prefixes

Prefix	Meaning	Examples	
ab–	away from	**ab**sent	**ab**domen
		abduct	**ab**hor
		abdicate	**ab**normal
ad–[1]	to, toward	**ad**vantage	**ag**gressive
		accept	**al**loy
		arrive	**at**tempt
circum–	around	**circum**stance	**circum**flex
		circumambient	**circum**locution
		circumcise	**circum**scribe
con–[2]	together, with	**con**tact	**col**lection
		corrupt	**com**bine
		coexist	**com**muter
contra–	against, opposite	**contra**dict	**contra**flow
		contraband	**contra**lateral
		contraceptive	**contra**pose
de–	down, about	**de**scend	**de**scent
		deduce	**de**moralize
		deport	**de**nounce
dis–[3]	apart, not	**dis**rupt	**di**vestment
		display	**di**ligent
		difficult	**dis**proportionate
ex–[4]	out of	**ex**pel	**e**volve
		elevate	**e**ruption
		effort	**ex**port
in–[5]	in, into, not	**im**pose	**il**logical
		imperfect	**ir**responsible
		impossible	**il**luminate

1   Assimilated Prefix
2   Assimilated Prefix
3   Assimilated Prefix
4   Assimilated Prefix
5   Assimilated Prefix

Prefix	Meaning	Examples	
inter-	between	**inter**state	**inter**mission
		interpreter	**inter**planetary
		international	**inter**course
intra-, intro-	within	**intro**vert	**intro**gression
		introduction	**intro**spective
		intravenous	**intra**cerebral
multi-	many	**multi**ple	**multi**cultural
		multiplication	**multi**directional
		multicasting	**multi**disciplinary
ob-[6]	against, in the way of	**ob**stacle	**op**posite
		obsolete	**of**fense
		occurrence	**oc**cidental
per-	through, entirely	**per**form	**per**centage
		perpendicular	**per**cussion
		permeate	
post-	after	**post**pone	**post**erior
		postnatal	**post**doctoral
		postnasal	**post**humous
pre-	before	**pre**dict	**pre**conceive
		prescription	**pre**frontal
		pretend	**pre**fer
pro-	forth, forward	**pro**cess	**pro**tractor
		promote	**pro**clamation
		production	**pro**gression
re-	back, again	**re**port	**re**position
		reduction	**re**vitalize
		relocate	**re**ferral
sub-[7]	under, below	**sub**merge	**suf**fering
		successful	**sub**ordinate
		supplement	**sup**portive
trans-	across	**trans**national	**trans**form
		translucent	**trans**mutation
		transmission	**trans**verse

6   Assimilated Prefix
7   Assimilated Prefix

appendix E. Greek Combining Forms

Combining Form	Meaning	Examples	
anthrop	man	anthropology anthropological philanthropy	anthropoid anthropomorphic misanthropy
apo	away	apostrophe apocalypse apogee	apoplexy apotheosis apocryphal
arch	chief	monarch architecture anarchy	monarchy oligarchy architect
archae	ancient	archaeology archaeologist archaeobotany	archaeoastronomy archaeopteryx archaeomagnetis
aut	self	automatic autism autograph	autopsy autocracy autonomous
baro	weight	barometer barograms barograph	barometric baroceptor barography
bibli	book	bibliography bibliophile bibliographer	bibliomania bibliomancy bible
bio	life	biology biofeedback bionic	symbiosis microbiology biopsy

Combining Form	Meaning	Examples	
cardio	heart	cardiologist cardiogram cardiovascular	cardiology cardiopulmonary cardiomyopathy
cata	down, against	cataract catalogue catastrophe	catapult catacomb catatonic
chrom	color	chromosome chromatin monochrome	polychrome flourochromes chromium
chron	time	chronometer chronometric chronology	chronograph synchronize chronicle
crat	rule	democrat autocrat bureaucrat	democratic plutocrat aristocrat
cycl	wheel	unicycle bicycle cycle	cyclist tricycle recycle
cyt	cells	cytoplasm hemocyte cytology	leukocyte cytochrome phagocyte
dem	people	democracy pandemic demography	democrat epidemic demagogue
derm	skin	pachyderm xeroderma hypodermic	ectoderm endoderm dermal
di	two	dimethyl dichotomy dicephalous	dipole dihydrogen oxide dicalcium
dia	through, across	diameter diabetes diagram	diagonal diatribe diaspora
dox	belief	orthodox unorthodox paradox	heterodox doxology ferredoxin

Combining Form	Meaning	Examples	
dys	difficulty	**dys**lexia **dys**calculia **dys**functional	**dys**graphia **dys**pepsia **dys**entery
endo	internal, inside	**endo**skeleton **endo**crine **endo**scope	**endo**plasm **endo**derm **endo**cardia
epi	on, over	**epi**dermis **epi**logue **epi**demic	**epi**lepsy **epi**cardium **epi**glottis
ethn	nation	**ethn**ocentric **ethn**ology **ethn**obotany	**ethn**ologist **ethn**ic **ethn**olinguistic
eu	good	**eu**logy **eu**calyptus **eu**genics	**eu**phony **eu**thanasia **eu**phemism
exo	outer, external	**exo**skeleton **exo**thermic **exo**dontics	**exo**cytosis **exo**dus
gam	marriage	mono**gam**y bi**gam**y poly**gam**y	mono**gam**ous bi**gam**ist poly**gam**ist
geo	earth	**geo**logy **geo**graphy **geo**metric	**geo**desic **geo**metry **geo**physics
gnos	knowledge	a**gnos**tic pro**gnos**is **gnos**is	dia**gnos**is **Gnos**ticism misdia**gnos**is
gon	angle	poly**gon** diag**on**al penta**gon**	trig**on**ometry octa**gon** hexa**gon**
gram, graph	write, draw	photo**graph** pro**gram** mono**gram**	auto**graph** bio**graph**y photo**graph**er
hem	blood	**hem**oglobin **hem**atology **hem**ostat	**hem**ocyte **hem**ophiliac **hem**orrhage

Combining Form	Meaning	Examples	
hemi	half	**hemi**sphere **hemi**cellulose **hemi**chordate	**hemi**cranial **hemi**colectomy **hemi**hydrate
hetero	different	**hetero**sexual **hetero**dox **hetero**geneous	**hetero**chromatic **hetero**chromosome **hetero**clite
homo	same	**homo**genize **homo**logous **homo**phone	**homo**nym **homo**zygous **homo**genous
hydr	water	**hydr**aulic **hydr**ophobia **hydr**ofoil	**hydr**oplane **hydr**ogen
hypn	sleep	**hypn**otize **hypn**otic **hypn**osis	**hypn**otherapy **hypn**otoxin **hypn**one
hypo	beneath	**hypo**dermic **hypo**crite **hypo**glycemic	**hypo**chondria **hypo**tonic **hypo**thesize
iatr	to heal	psych**iatr**y ped**iatr**ics ger**iatr**ics	psych**iatr**ist pod**iatr**y ped**iatr**ician
iso	equal, similar	**iso**sceles **iso**bar **iso**mer	**iso**tope **iso**metric **iso**butene
kine	movement	**kine**sthetic **kine**tic **kine**siology	**kine**matic **kine**sis **kine**scope
lex	words	**lex**icon dys**lex**ia **lex**icography	**lex**is **lex**icology **lex**igraphy
lith	stone	mono**lith** **lith**osphere **lith**ology	**lith**ography **lith**oid **lith**otomy
logy	study of	bio**logy** geo**logy** zoo**logy**	climato**logy** dermato**logy** crimino**logy**

Combining Form	Meaning	Examples	
macro	large	**macro**cosm **macro**n **macro**biotics	**macro**graph **macro**instruction **macro**media
meter, metry	measure	thermo**meter** speedo**meter** geo**metry**	seismo**meter** chrono**meter** trigono**metry**
micro	small	**micro**cosm **micro**graph **micro**biology	**micro**meter **micro**wave **micro**phone
mono	one	**mono**gram **mono**theistic **mono**nucleosis	**mono**cle **mono**atomic **mono**carboxylic
morph	change, form	**morph**ology a**morph**ous ecto**morph**	proto**morph**ic poly**morph**ous anthropo**morph**ic
neo	new	**neo**phyte **neo**classic **neo**logism	**neo**colonialism **Neo**lithic
neur	nerve	**neur**osurgeon **neur**otic **neur**ology	**neur**on **neur**opathology **neur**ological
nym	name	pseudo**nym** homo**nym** crypto**nym**	hetero**nym** syno**nym**ous ano**nym**ous
orth	straight	**orth**odox **orth**odontic **orth**otics	**orth**opedic **orth**ostatic **orth**ographic
osis	disease	necr**osis** osm**osis** psych**osis**	trichin**osis** metamorph**osis** diagn**osis**
paleo	old, ancient	**paleo**ntology **Paleo**zoic **paleo**ntologist	**paleo**astronomy **paleo**botany **paleo**climatology
pan	all	**pan**acea **pan**theon **pan**demic	**pan**oply **pan**demonium **pan**orama

Combining Form	Meaning	Examples	
para	beside, beyond	**para**normal **para**psychology **para**llel	**para**noia **para**bola **para**site
path	feeling	sym**path**y anti**path**y **path**etic	**path**ologist tele**path**y **path**ological
penta	five	**penta**gon **penta**gram **penta**meter	**penta**cle **penta**d **penta**dactyl
phil	love	**Phil**adelphia **phil**anthropy **phil**osophy	**phil**anderer **phil**harmonic **phil**ogynist
phobia	intense fear	hydro**phobia** acro**phobia** xeno**phobia**	agora**phobia** necro**phobia** claustro**phobia**
phon	sound, voice	**phon**ograph **phon**eme caco**phon**y	tele**phon**e **phon**ology sym**phon**y
phot	light	**phot**ograph **phot**ographer **phot**ogenic	**phot**osynthesis **phot**okinetic **phot**on
physi	nature	**physi**cian **physi**cs **physi**ology	**physi**cal **physi**ological **physi**otherapy
polic, polis, polit	city	**polit**ician **polic**y **polic**e	metro**polis** cosmo**polit**an metro**polit**an
poly	many	**poly**gamy mono**poly** **poly**gon	**poly**ethylene **poly**ester **poly**chromatic
proto	first	**proto**type **proto**plasm **proto**binary	**proto**zoan **proto**lithic **proto**morphic
psych	mind, soul	**psych**opathic **psych**ic **psych**otic	**psych**opath **psych**iatry **psych**otherapy

Combining Form	Meaning	Examples	
saur	lizard	dino**saur**	dilopho**saur**us
		tyranno**saur**us rex	brachio**saur**us
		corytho**saur**us	styraco**saur**us
scop	to see	tele**scop**e	micro**scop**ic
		peri**scop**e	echo**scop**e
		arthro**scop**ic	
soph	wisdom	**soph**omore	philo**soph**y
		sophisticated	**soph**omoric
		sophist	**soph**istry
spher	round shape	atmo**spher**e	**spher**oid
		hemi**spher**e	tropo**spher**e
		iono**spher**e	hydro**spher**e
techn	skill	**techn**ical	**techn**ostructure
		technology	**techn**ophile
		technophobia	**techn**ological
tele	distant, far	**tele**phone	**tele**graph
		telemetry	**tele**type
		telepathy	**tele**kinetic
theo	God	**theo**logy	**theo**morphic
		theophobia	**theo**cracy
		theosophy	**theo**centric
therm	heat	**therm**al	**therm**odynamics
		thermostat	**therm**os
		thermometer	endo**therm**ic
tox	poison	**tox**ic	**tox**icity
		in**tox**icate	**tox**icology
		de**tox**ification	**tox**in
xeno	stranger	**xeno**phobia	**xeno**diagnosis
		xenophile	**xeno**transplant
		xenobiotic	
xer	dryness	**xer**odermia	**xer**ostomia
		xeroderma	**xer**osis
		xeromorphic	**xer**oradiography

Assessment of Sound/Symbol Correspondence

T H E   purpose of the Assessment of Sound/ Symbol Correspondence (ASSC) is to provide parents with a tangible record of the phonograms that present as problematic for their children. The idea is to use the assessment as a guide to determine where to focus the initial remediation. Ideally, parents will want to lead their children through the entire language training system; however, the assessment is designed to identify gaps that impede academic progress in reading and spelling.

The administration of the assessment is fairly straightforward. First, three copies of the assessment should be made. Parents are encouraged to administer one assessment at the beginning of language training, one in the middle, and one after parents have determined that remediation or primary instruction has served its purpose successfully.

The parent should take the Recording Form and give the student the Reading Form. Students are to give the sound of the phonograms on the Reading Form by reading the phonograms vertically, from top to bottom. Many of the phonograms have multiple sounds. If the student only gives one sound for phonograms with multiple sounds, parents may ask the student if there are any additional sounds made by the phonograms.

If a student does not know the sounds represented by any of the phonograms, please let him know that this is okay. He should merely state, "I don't know." This serves as valuable information and will guide the parent in remediation.

After the assessment is completed, fill in the appropriate tally on the front of the Assessment Form. Keep the tally in an accessible place. Refer to it often as you design your lesson plans.

Assessment of Sound/ Symbol Correspondence

Administration Form

Student Name: _____ Date of Assessment: _____

School: _____ Grade: _____ Age: _____

Examiner: _____

Reason for Referral: _____

_____

_____

Family history of language-based learning issues? _____

_____

_____

Vowels:	_____ /14	Consonants:	_____ /27
Vowel Teams:	_____ /34	"R" Controlled Vowels:	_____ /5
Initial Blends:	_____ /25	Final Blends:	_____ /14
Consonant Digraphs:	_____ /9	Special Phonograms:	_____ /20
Consonant + "le":	_____ /11	Vowel + Consonant + Consonant:	
Final Stable Syllables:	_____ /38		_____ /11

Assessment of Sound/Symbol Correspondence

Recording Form

Vowels	Vowel Sounds	Consonants	Consonant Sounds	Consonants	Consonant Sounds
a	/ ā / _____	b	/ b / _____	p	/ p / _____
a	/ ă / _____	c	/ k / _____	qu	/ kw / _____
a	/ aw / _____	c	/ s / _____	qu	/ k / _____
e	/ ē / _____	d	/ d / _____	que	/ k / _____
e	/ ĕ / _____	f	/ f / _____	r	/ r / _____
i	/ ī / _____	g	/ g / _____	s	/ s / _____
i	/ ĭ / _____	g	/ j / _____	s	/ z / _____
i	/ ē / _____	h	/ h / _____	t	/ t / _____
o	/ ō / _____	j	/ j / _____	v	/ v / _____
o	/ ŏ / _____	k	/ k / _____	w	/ w / _____
u	/ ū / _____	l	/ l / _____	x	/ ks / _____
u	/ ŭ / _____	m	/ m / _____	x	/ gz / _____
u	/ oo / _____	n	/ n / _____	x	/ z / _____
y	/ ī / _____			z	/ z / _____

Vowel Teams	Vowel Team Sounds	Vowel Teams	Vowel Team Sounds	Vowel Teams	Vowel Team Sounds
a-e	/ ā / _____	ei	/ ā / _____	oi	/ ō ē / _____
ai	/ ā / _____	eigh	/ ā / _____	oo	/ oo / _____
au	/ aw / _____	eu	/ ū / _____	oo	/ oo / _____
aw	/ aw / _____	eu	/ oo / _____	ou	/ ŏ oo / _____
ay	/ ā / _____	ew	/ ū / _____	ou	/ oo / _____
ea	/ ē / _____	ew	/ oo / _____	ow	/ ō / _____
ea	/ ĕ / _____	ey	/ ē / _____	ow	/ ŏ oo / _____
ea	/ ā / _____	ey	/ ā / _____	oy	/ ō ē / _____
e-e	/ ē / _____	i-e	/ ī / _____	ue	/ ū / _____
ee	/ ē / _____	igh	/ ī / _____	ue	/ oo / _____
ei	/ ē / _____	oa	/ ō / _____		
		oe	/ ō / _____		
		o-e	/ ō / _____		

Initial Blends	Initial Blend Sounds	Initial Blends	Initial Blend Sounds	Final Blends	Final Blend Sounds
bl-	/ bl / _____	sk-	/ sk / _____	-ct	/ kt / _____
br-	/ br / _____	sl-	/ sl / _____	-ft	/ ft / _____
cl-	/ cl / _____	sm-	/ sm / _____	-lk	/ lk / _____
cr-	/ cr / _____	sn-	/ sn / _____	-mpt	/ mpt / _____
fl-	/ fl / _____	sp-	/ sp / _____	-nch	/ nch / _____
fr-	/ fr / _____	spl-	/ spl / _____	-nct	/ nct / _____
gl-	/ gl / _____	spr-	/ spr / _____	-nd	/ nd / _____
gr-	/ gr / _____	squ-	/ skw / _____	-ng	/ ng / _____
pl-	/ pl / _____	st-	/ st / _____	-nk	/ nk / _____
pr-	/ pr / _____	str-	/ str / _____	-nt	/ nt / _____
sc-	/ sk / _____	thr-	/ thr / _____	-pt	/ pt / _____
scr-	/ skr / _____	tr-	/ tr / _____	-sk	/ sk / _____
shr-	/ shr / _____			-sp	/ sp / _____
				-st	/ st / _____

"R"-Controlled Vowels	"R"-Controlled Vowel Sounds	Special Phonograms	Special Phonogram Sounds	Consonant Digraphs	Consonant Digraph Sounds
ar	/ aw er / _____	-ci-	/ sh / _____	ch	/ ch / _____
er	/ er / _____	-ci-	/ ch / _____	ch	/ k / _____
ir	/ er / _____	-du-	/ joo / _____	ch	/ sh / _____
or	/ ō er / _____	-dge	/ j / _____	ck	/ k / _____
ur	/ er / _____	-ed	/ ŏd / _____	ph	/ f / _____
		-ed	/ d / _____	sh	/ sh / _____
		-ed	/ t / _____	th	/ th / _____
		gh	/ g / _____	th	/ th / _____
		gn	/ n / _____	wh	/ hw / _____
		kn-	/ n / _____		
		-mb	/ m / _____		
		-mn	/ m / _____		
		rh-	/ r / _____		
		-si-	/ sh / _____		
		-si-	/ zh / _____		

(continued on p. 224)

"R"-Controlled Vowels	"R"-Controlled Vowel Sounds	Special Phonograms	Special Phonogram Sounds	Consonant Digraphs	Consonant Digraph Sounds
		-tch	/ ch / _____		
		-ti-	/ sh / _____		
		-ti-	/ ch / _____		
		-tu-	/ ch<u>oo</u> / _____		
		wr-	/ r / _____		

Consonant + "le"	Consonant + "le" Sounds	Vowel + Consonant + Consonant	Vowel + Consonant + Consonant Sounds
-ble	/ bəl / _____	-ald	/ awld / _____
-cle	/ kəl / _____	-alk	/ awk / _____
-ckle	/ kəl / _____	-all	/ awl / _____
-dle	/ dəl / _____	-alt	/ awlt / _____
-fle	/ fəl / _____	-ild	/ īld / _____
-gle	/ gəl / _____	-ind	/ īnd / _____
-kle	/ kəl / _____	-ind	/ ĭnd / _____
-ple	/ pəl / _____	-old	/ ōld / _____
-stle	/ səl / _____	-oll	/ ōl / _____
-tle	/ təl / _____	-olt	/ ōlt / _____
-zle	/ zəl / _____	-ost	/ ōst / _____

Final Stable Syllables	Final Stable Syllable Sounds	Final Stable Syllables	Final Stable Syllable Sounds
-able	/ ə bəl / _____	-ery	/ ər ē / _____
-ade	/ ād / _____	-ful	/ fəl / _____
-age	/ ĭ j / _____	-fully	/ fəl ē / _____
-al	/ ə l / _____	-hood	/ hood / _____
-ain	/ ĭ n / _____	-ible	/ ə bəl / _____
-ance	/ əns / _____	-ing	/ ēng / _____
-ancy	/ ənsē / _____	-ite	/ ī t / _____
-ane	/ ān / _____	-ive	/ ī v / _____
-ant	/ ənt / _____	-less	/ lĕs / _____

Final Stable Syllables	Final Stable Syllable Sounds	Final Stable Syllables	Final Stable Syllable Sounds
-ary	/ ā ər ē / _____	-ly	/ lē / _____
-ary	/ ər ē / _____	-ment	/ mĕnt / _____
-ate	/ āt / _____	-ness	/ nĕs / _____
-cial	/ shəl / _____	-ory	/ ō ər ē / _____
-cian	/ shən / _____	-ous	/ əs / _____
-ciate	/ shē āt / _____	-sion	/ shən / _____
-cient	/ shənt / _____	-sion	/ zhən / _____
-el	/ əl / _____	-tion	/ shən / _____
-ence	/ əns / _____	-tion	/ chən / _____
-ent	/ ənt / _____	-ture	/ chər / _____

Assessment of Sound/Symbol Correspondence

Reading Form

Vowels

a	o
e	u
i	y

Consonants

b	p
c	qu
d	que
f	r
g	s
h	t
j	v
k	w
l	x
m	z
n	

Vowel Teams

a-e	ey
ai	i-e
au	igh
aw	oa
ay	oe
ea	o-e
e-e	oi
ee	oo
ei	ou
eigh	ow
eu	oy
ew	ue

Initial Blends

bl–	sk–
br–	sl–
cl–	sm–
cr–	sn–
fl–	sp–
fr–	spl–
gl–	spr–
gr–	squ–
pl–	st–
pr–	str–
sc–	thr–
scr–	tr–
shr–	

Final Blends

–ct	–ng
–ft	–nk
–lk	–nt
–mpt	–pt
–nch	–sk
–nct	–sp
–nd	–st

"R"-Controlled Vowels

ar   or

er   ur

ir

Special Phonograms

-ci-   -mn

-du-   rh-

-dge   -si-

-ed   -tch

gh   -ti-

gn   -tu-

kn-   wr-

-mb

Consonant Digraphs

ch   sh

ck   th

ph   wh

Consonant + "le"

-ble	-kle
-cle	-ple
-ckle	-stle
-dle	-tle
-fle	-zle
-gle	

Vowel + Consonant + Consonant

-ald	-ind
-alk	-old
-all	-oll
-alt	-olt
-ild	-ost

Final Stable Syllables

-able	-ery
-ade	-ful
-age	-fully
-al	-hood
-ain	-ible
-ance	-ing
-ancy	-ite
-ane	-ive
-ant	-less
-ary	-ly
-ate	-ment
-cial	-ness
-cian	-ory
-ciate	-ous
-cient	-sion
-el	-tion
-ence	-ture
-ent	

Spelling Deck Administration Form

CLEARLY say each word to the student. Then, read the sentence that includes the word. Finally, repeat the word.

1.	ceiling	The **ceiling** is very high.
2.	belief	That is my **belief**.
3.	sneaker	I can't find my **sneaker**.
4.	market	This little piggy went to **market**.
5.	confuse	I don't want to **confuse** you.
6.	handshake	You have a firm **handshake**.
7.	misjudge	You may **misjudge** my strengths.
8.	patched	Mom **patched** my jeans.
9.	applaud	I **applaud** your efforts.
10.	postpone	Maybe we should **postpone** our meeting.
11.	stable	She is a very **stable** person.
12.	scissors	You cut paper with **scissors**.
13.	squeamish	The blood made me **squeamish**.
14.	pony	I liked riding the **pony**.
15.	lucky	I am a **lucky** guy.
16.	extreme	Your reaction was **extreme**.

17. gargle — I **gargle** with mouthwash.

18. juice — May I have some more **juice**?

19. necktie — Dad lost his **necktie**.

20. chorus — Mom sings in a **chorus**.

21. feudal — That is a **feudal** society.

22. thirsty — Exercise will make you **thirsty**.

23. immerse — Should I **immerse** my rubber duckie in the bathtub?

24. daybreak — I'll return before **daybreak**.

25. spider — Little Miss Muffet was scared by a **spider**.

26. freedom — **Freedom** is a great thing to have.

27. eighteen — My sister is **eighteen**.

28. symbol — A statue is a **symbol**.

29. reindeer — Rudolph is a red-nosed **reindeer**.

30. baby — I used to be a **baby**.

31. whistle — Do you know how to **whistle**?

32. sniffle — I **sniffle** when I have a cold.

33. quality — That car is of high **quality**.

34. ointment — Mom put **ointment** on my cut.

35. pillow — I have a soft **pillow**.

36. freestyle — I won the **freestyle** swimming event.

37. dismay — Much to my **dismay**, Santa didn't come.

38. complain — I don't like to **complain**.

39. sewer — David fell in a **sewer** drain.

40. midnight — I stayed up past **midnight**.

41. spongy — Angel food cake is **spongy**.

42. allow — Dad won't **allow** me to have a motorcycle.

43.	bouncing	Kelly is **bouncing** on the bed.
44.	youthful	She has a **youthful** appearance.
45.	argue	We **argue** all of the time.
46.	threaten	They **threaten** me during lunch.
47.	bemoan	I **bemoan** having to leave a fun party.
48.	backhoe	They dug the hole with a **backhoe**.
49.	survey	The man is taking a **survey**.
50.	recite	Do you want me to **recite** a poem?
51.	typhoon	I was scared by the **typhoon**.
52.	distort	Don't **distort** what I said.
53.	music	I love country **music**.
54.	rolled	Jack and Jill **rolled** down the hill.
55.	valley	We live in a **valley**.
56.	childhood	I have many **childhood** memories.
57.	bluffing	I think he was **bluffing**.
58.	secret	Don't tell anyone my **secret**.
59.	mushroom	Alice ate a **mushroom**.
60.	curfew	We have a **curfew** tonight.
61.	mustache	Your **mustache** tickles.
62.	beggar	Halloween turns a child into a **beggar**.
63.	dawdle	We don't have time for you to **dawdle**.

Diagnostic Deck Assessment Form

Date of Diagnostic	Correct in Reading	Correct in Spelling	Dates Reviewed	Diagnostic Word
				ceiling
				belief
				sneaker
				market
				confuse
				handshake
				misjudge
				patched
				applaud
				postpone
				stable
				scissors
				squeamish
				pony
				lucky

Date of Diagnostic	Correct in Reading	Correct in Spelling	Dates Reviewed	Diagnostic Word
				extreme
				gargle
				juice
				necktie
				chorus
				feudal
				thirsty
				immerse
				daybreak
				spider
				freedom
				eighteen
				symbol
				reindeer
				baby
				whistle
				sniffle
				quality
				ointment
				pillow
				freestyle
				dismay
				complain
				sewer
				midnight
				spongy

Date of Diagnostic	Correct in Reading	Correct in Spelling	Dates Reviewed	Diagnostic Word
				allow
				bouncing
				youthful
				argue
				threaten
				bemoan
				backhoe
				survey
				recite
				typhoon
				distort
				music
				rolled
				valley
				childhood
				bluffing
				secret
				mushroom
				curfew
				mustache
				beggar
				dawdle

About the Author

Walter E. Dunson, Ph.D., is the founder and executive director of The English Code Language Training System, a company that provides language remediation services to students with language acquisition difficulties. He is a former member of the Board of Directors of the International Dyslexia Association (Houston Branch) and has authored four books.

Index